THE FINALISTS

A Graphical Lookback at Trinidad & Tobago's Calypso and Soca Monarch Finals

Part 2

Written and Compiled by John E. H. Barry

Copyright © 2017 by John E. H. Barry
All rights reserved
No part of this book may be reproduced or transmitted in any form or by any means electronic or mechanical including photocopying, recording, or by any information storage and retrieval system, without permission in writing from the publisher.

ISBN 978-976-8271-54-9
John E. H. Barry
#4 Exchange Lots
Couva
Trinidad and Tobago
2017

Printed in Trinidad and Tobago by C.S. Printers and Design

Cover Design by Christian Smart

CONTENTS

Acknowledgements	I
Foreword	II
International Groovy Soca Monarch Competition 2005 - 2015	1
International Power Soca Monarch Competition 2007 – 2015	25
National Calypso Monarch Competition 2007 - 2016	53
Appendix A	
(i) A Profile of the Placing in the National/International Power Soca Monarch Finals	89
(ii) A Profile of the Placing in the National Calypso King/Monarch Finals	95
(iii) A Profile of the Placing in the Groovy Soca Monarch Finals	100
Appendix B: Streaks	
(i) A Breakdown of Consecutive Appearances in the National/International Power Soca Monarch Finals	103
(ii) A Breakdown of Consecutive Appearances in the National Calypso King/Monarch Finals	105
(iii) A Breakdown of Consecutive Appearances in the Groovy Soca Monarch Finals	108
Appendix C	
(i) A Score Sheet of Appearances in the National/International Power Soca Monarch Finals	109
(ii) A Score Sheet of Appearances in the National Calypso King/Monarch Finals	111
(iii) A Score Sheet of Appearances in the Groovy Soca Monarch Finals	113
Appendix D	
(i) A Profile of the National/International Power Soca Monarch Winners	114
(ii) A Profile of the National Calypso King/Monarch Winners	115
(iii) A Profile of the Groovy Soca Monarch Winners	117
Bibliography	118

Acknowledgements

I owe a debt of gratitude to a number of people whose support, assistance and guidance propelled me to the completion of this book. To my good friend, Steve Gellineau, for always allowing me to tap into his wealth of calypso knowledge. To the easy going Shawn Randoo who allowed me unlimited access to his cultural treasure trove. I am grateful to Wayne "Kassman" Mc Donald and Devon Seale of TUCO for their kind assistance when I needed to cross reference my information with the official records. Similarly to Janelle Phillip of Caribbean Prestige Foundation for the Performing Arts for being equally accommodating each time I called on her for information regarding the International Soca Monarch Competition. Special thanks to Dr. Hollis Liverpool—The Mighty Chalkdust—and Zeno Obi Constance for spending the time it took perusing their personal archives in search of information I knew I could get only from them respectively. To Gary "Afroman" Cardinez for putting the time and effort it took locating the specific photos I requested. To George Sambrano who guided me in the right direction each time I called. Thanks to Nicola Barriteau who was helpful with info on the Antigua and Barbuda soca scene. To Ray Funk for his timely suggestions which contributed to a more attractive product. Emile Borde, brother of Bianca Borde a.k.a. Buzzing Bee; thank you Emile for the rare photo. Thanks to Val Cuffy of Dominica for setting the record straight on questions I had about the soca scene in his land. I am greatly indebted to Edward Teddy Pinheiro, Josephine Torrel-Brown and Dianne Holdip for proof-reading the manuscript. Finally, my deepest gratitude to my family for their unstinting love and support.

Foreword

The Finalists Part 2 picks up from where Part 1 ends at 2006 with the International Soca Monarch and the Trinidad and Tobago National Calypso Monarch Competitions. In this edition the Groovy Soca Monarch Competition is added and the timelines are extended to 2016. The format is consistent with that of **Part 1**, as well as the objective of making available to the public a comprehensive account of the competitions presented. As the title of the book suggests, the focus is on the final night of each competition. Every finalist of the respective competitions staged each year is presented as well as the order in which they performed and the full placing, dashing away the established norm, even to this day, of making mention of just the top three places when presenting the results. This effort is stymied somewhat with respect to the results of the Soca Monarch competitions where from 2010 onward the governing body, at the request of the artistes, elected to release the placing of just the top four. Suffice it to say that by that measure the Soca Monarch results presented here are to be considered "full and complete".

The Groovy Soca Monarch Competition was introduced in 2005 and discontinued after the 2015 carnival season. The relatively short history of that competition is fully captured in this edition. Moving forward to 2016, the Soca Monarch scene has reverted to the single-competition format as it was at its inception and as a natural progression the terms "Power Soca" and "Groovy Soca" were dropped. The finalists, all pitted against each other once again in one grand showdown, have enabled the completion of a cycle. Caribbean Prestige Foundation for the Performing Arts, the governing body for the Soca Monarch Competition, hit the reset button in 2016, serving up at the same time a few new and hopefully progressive ideas for the administration of the competition.

An important aspect of the information presented in this book is the varying dimensions of research and analytical perspectives being made available. On one level it serves as a reliable source of reference data for those who need it at hand and at a glance. Throughout the book there is also a presentation of related facts and factoids which in some instances point to the extracurricular activities of certain artistes. For those seeking a higher level of engagement with the information there are avenues for a deeper and more focused analysis of selected issues such as the performance profile of a particular artiste or group of artistes, the examination of trends, administrative policy adjustments and the influence of politics on our cultural expressions, among so many others. In the general sense the book presents a bird's eye view of how each competition has meandered through the years creating its own history.

The Groovy Soca Finals
2005 - 2015

International Groovy Soca Monarch Competition 2005

Date: Friday 4th February
Venue: Queen's Park Oval, St. Clair, Trinidad and Tobago

Order of Appearance

	Artiste	Country
1	Lil' Bitts	Trinidad and Tobago
2	Johnny King	Trinidad and Tobago
3	Keishea Stewart	Trinidad and Tobago
4	Nesta Boxhill	Trinidad and Tobago
5	Michelle Sylvester	Trinidad and Tobago
6	H20 Flo	Trinidad and Tobago
7	Mini Priest	Trinidad and Tobago
8	Jamsie P	St. Vincent and the Grenadines
9	Blackie	Trinidad and Tobago

Results

Place	Artiste	Song
1	Michelle Sylvester	Somebody's Sleeping In Your Bed
2	H2O Phlo	Come Baby
3	Blackie	Ah Hook
4	Mini Priest	Body Water
5	Keishea Stewart	Pack Your Things And Go
6	Jamsie P	Nookie
7	Johnny King	No Other But You
8	Lil' Bitts	Crush
9	Nesta Boxhill	Cool Meh Down

Places 6 to 9 are unconfirmed.

Michelle Sylvester also won the Soca Queen Competition which was held on the night before she won the Groovy Soca Monarch Competition.

Nesta Boxhill is now known as Sekon Sta.

Blazer was slated to sing in the number 2 position, but did not take the stage.

Michelle Sylvester
Photo provided by TriniSoca.com

2007

Date: Friday 16th February
Venue: National Stadium, Woodbrook, Trinidad & Tobago

Order of Appearance

	Artiste	Country
1	Blackie	Trinidad and Tobago
2	Blazer Dan	Trinidad and Tobago
3	Nnika	Grenada
4	Fireball	Trinidad and Tobago
5	Biggie Irie	Barbados
6	Nadia Batson	Trinidad and Tobago
7	Crazy	Trinidad and Tobago
8	Shurwayne Winchester	Trinidad and Tobago
9	Patrice Roberts	Trinidad and Tobago
10	Chucky	Trinidad and Tobago
11	Terry Seales	Trinidad and Tobago
12	Umi Marcano	Trinidad and Tobago

Results

Place	Artiste	Song
1	Biggie Irie	We Nah Going Home
2	Chucky	Turn Around
3	Nadia Batson	Caribbean Girl
4	Shurwayne Winchester	Allequa
5	Patrice Roberts	Sugar Boy
6	Crazy	Cold Sweat
7	Terry Seales	Seduction
8	Blackie	Confessions
9	Blazer Dan	Be Mine Tonight
10	Fireball	What I Want
11	Nnika	Don't Let Me Go
12	Umi Marcano	Move That Body

Biggie Irie became the first non-Trinbagonian monarch (Groovy or Power) in the history of the competition. This was his debut on the International Soca Monarch stage.

Biggie Irie
Photo provided by TriniSoca.com

Chucky was the winner of the 2007 Stars of Tomorrow Calypso Competition; he sang "Street Justice." This competition is staged by the National Youth Action Committee, the youth arm of the National Joint Action Committee which is the parent body overseeing other competitions such as the Young Kings Calypso Monarch Competition and the Calypso Queen Competition among others. Chucky placed second in the Young Kings Calypso Monarch Competition, again singing "Street Justice".

Umi Marcano was allowed automatic entry into the Groovy Soca Monarch Finals as part of his prize for winning the Synergy Soca Star Competition. This was a soca singing competition staged annually by Synergy TV to unearth and nurture young talent in Trinidad and Tobago. Synergy TV is a music oriented cable television channel located in Woodbrook, on the outskirts of Port of Spain, Trinidad and Tobago.

Calypsonian Crazy enjoyed an outstanding and hectic campaign throughout the 2007 carnival season. The then sixty-two year old found crossover success with "Cold Sweat", thrilling audiences nightly at the Revue Calypso Tent and leaving audiences wanting more on the party circuit where he was in demand at every major fete. The icing on the carnival cake for him was finding himself among the finalists at both the National Calypso Monarch and Groovy Soca Monarch Competitions (see page 56).

2008

Date: Friday 1st February
Venue: Queen's Park Oval, St. Clair, Trinidad & Tobago

Order of Appearance

	Artiste	Country
1	Patrice Roberts	Trinidad and Tobago
2	Farmer Nappy	Trinidad and Tobago
3	OG	Trinidad and Tobago
4	Peter C. Lewis	Trinidad and Tobago
5	Tony Prescott	Trinidad and Tobago
6	Shurwayne Winchester	Trinidad and Tobago
7	Tizzy	Antigua and Barbuda
8	Biggie Irie	Barbados
9	Skhi	Trinidad and Tobago
10	Mr. Dale	Barbados
11	Kerwin Du Bois & Shal Marshall	Trinidad and Tobago

Results

Place	Artiste	Song
1	Shurwayne Winchester	Carnival Please Stay
2	Patrice Roberts	More Wuk
3	Kerwin Du Bois & Shal Marshall	Gal Farm
4	Farmer Nappy	Chippin
5	Mr. Dale	Soca Junkie
6	Skhi	Desire
7	Tony Prescott	Wine Low
8	Peter C. Lewis	Over And Over
9	Biggie Irie	Band On Fire
10	Tizzy	Kick It Off
11	OG	Roll It

OG gained automatic entry into finals having won the 2008 Synergy Soca Star Competition.

2009

Date: Friday 20th February
Venue: National Stadium, Woodbrook, Trinidad & Tobago

Order of Appearance

	Artiste	Country
1	Tizzy & Richard Trumpet	Antigua and Barbuda/Trinidad and Tobago
2	Patch & Mastermind	Trinidad and Tobago
3	Hunter	Trinidad and Tobago
4	Zoelah	St. Vincent and The Grenadines
5	Biggie Irie	Barbados
6	Nadia Batson	Trinidad and Tobago
7	Fay Ann Lyons-Alvarez	Trinidad and Tobago
8	Zan	Trinidad and Tobago
9	Shurwayne Winchester	Trinidad and Tobago
10	Kerwin Du Bois	Trinidad and Tobago
11	Benjai	Trinidad and Tobago

Results

Place	Artiste	Song
1	Fay Ann Lyons-Alvarez	Heavy T Bumper
2	Shurwayne Winchester	Make It Yours
3	Benjai	Drunk Again
4	Zoelah	Wine Up On Me
5	Biggie Irie	Big Girlz
6	Kerwin Du Bois	Two Days
7	Nadia Batson	Bumpers Rule
8	Tizzy & Richard Trumpet	Wuk Meh
9	Hunter	Jep Sting Naina
10	Zan	Slip Away
11	Patch & Mastermind	Rum & Roti

A broad interpretation of the Heavy T Bumper theme was served up to the audience on Fantastic Friday with the inclusion of contestants from the Miss Big and Beautiful Pageant and the queen of the calypso world, Calypso Rose, each playing their respective roles as components of Fay Ann's stage presentation. She etched her name indelibly in the annals of soca history by making a clean sweep of all the prizes she could have possibly won in the carnival season. These include the Groovy Soca Monarch, Power Soca Monarch, People's Choice Monarch and the Road March titles. She became the second artiste to sweep both Power and Groovy Soca Monarch titles, (Shurwayne Winchester was the first in 2006), and the first to sweep Power, Groovy and People's Choice on Fantastic Friday. Fay Ann gave birth to her first, and to date, only child just one week after the Soca Monarch Finals (see page 30).

2010

Date: Friday, 12th February
Venue: Queen's Park Oval, St Clair, Trinidad & Tobago

Order of Appearance

	Artiste	Country
1	Ainsley King	Trinidad and Tobago
2	Nnika Francis	Grenada
3	Metro	Trinidad and Tobago
4	Rikki Jai	Trinidad and Tobago
5	Chucky	Trinidad and Tobago
6	Shurwayne Winchester	Trinidad and Tobago
7	Patrice Roberts	Trinidad and Tobago
8	Fay Ann Lyons-Alvarez	Trinidad and Tobago
9	TC	Barbados
10	Zoelah	St. Vincent and The Grenadines
11	Lil' Bitts	Trinidad and Tobago
12	Kerwin Du Bois and Farmer Nappy	Trinidad and Tobago
13	KMC	Trinidad and Tobago

Results

Place	Artiste	Song
1	Shurwayne Winchester	Murdah
2	Fay Ann Lyons-Alvarez	Start Wining
3	Rikki Jai	Barman
4	Patrice Roberts	J'Ouvert Jam
NOT DISCLOSED	Zoelah	More Water
NOT DISCLOSED	Kerwin Du Bois and Farmer Nappy	Pavement
NOT DISCLOSED	Nnika Francis	Survivor
NOT DISCLOSED	Lil' Bitts	Careful
NOT DISCLOSED	Chucky	Driffin
NOT DISCLOSED	Ainsley King	Bawl Out
NOT DISCLOSED	Metro	Streets of Trinidad
NOT DISCLOSED	TC	Hot Sun and Rhythm
NOT DISCLOSED	KMC	Nah Bad Talk Man

In 2010 text voting was introduced to the Soca Monarch Competition as part of the adjudication process allowing fans to play an active role in deciding who wins the respective crowns. Under that system votes texted in by the fans accounted for 35 percent of the artiste's final score while points awarded by the official judges accounted for 65 percent. Since then there has been some variation to this arrangement, by 2014 votes texted in accounted for just 5 percent of the final score.

Metro gained automatic entry into the finals having won the 2010 Synergy Soca Star Competition.

Ainsley King is the Chairman of the Tobago branch of the Trinbago Unified Calypsonians Organisation (TUCO). He is the younger brother of veteran calypsonian Johnny King.

2011

Date: Friday 4th March
Venue: National Stadium, Woodbrook, Trinidad & Tobago

Order of Appearance

	Artiste	Country
1	Ras Star	Trinidad and Tobago
2	Jahmoun	Trinidad and Tobago
3	Yankee Boy and Patch	Trinidad and Tobago
4	Megan Walrond	Trinidad and Tobago
5	Blaxx	Trinidad and Tobago
6	All Rounder	Trinidad and Tobago
7	Shurwayne Winchester	Trinidad and Tobago
8	Destra	Trinidad and Tobago
9	Chucky	Trinidad and Tobago
10	Benjai	Trinidad and Tobago
11	Denise Belfon	Trinidad and Tobago
12	Patrice Roberts	Trinidad and Tobago
13	Kerwin Du Bois	Trinidad and Tobago
14	Kees	Trinidad and Tobago
15	Cassi	Trinidad and Tobago

Results

Place	Artiste	Song
1	Kees	Wotless
2	Benjai	Trini
3	Destra	Cool It Down
4	Blaxx	Tanti Woi
NOT DISCLOSED	Patrice Roberts	Mas And Wining
NOT DISCLOSED	Chucky	My Bad Thing
NOT DISCLOSED	All Rounder	Body Wine
NOT DISCLOSED	Yankee Boy and Patch	Head Nice
NOT DISCLOSED	Jahmoun	Flashing Lights

Place	Artiste	Song
NOT DISCLOSED	Ras Star	Soca Fire
	Shurwayne Winchester	Paradising
	Cassi	Town Ting
	Kerwin Du Bois	Ah Ting
	Megan Walrond	Posse
	Denise Belfon	Dance & Dingolay

"Wotless" was by far the grooviest of the groovy in 2011; this tune was written and produced by Kerwin Du Bois. Kees The Band is credited as co-writer. Du Bois has without doubt proven his mettle as a singer of both calypso and soca, but has also emerged as a prolific producer/songwriter with an extensive string of hits credited to his name. As a finalist at the 2011 Soca Monarch Competition he found himself pitted against his own work, and as fate would have it he performed immediately before Kees Dieffenthaller's "Wotless" performance. "Ah Ting" was also one of the big hits of the season and although Du Bois competed as a solo act the recorded version of this song is a collaboration between him and Kes The Band. It was written and produced by Du Bois with co-writer credit also going to Kes The Band.

With two of the season's biggest hits, "Trini" and "Wine To The Side", Benjai enjoyed what arguably was his most successful carnival season to date. There was hardly a carnival event of note that didn't include him. Amid the revelry he entered and won the Young Kings Calypso Monarch Competition (TT$100,000 prize), banked a healthy TT$225,000 for securing second place in the Groovy Soca Monarch Competition, and an additional TT$60,000 for his twelfth spot in the National Calypso Monarch Finals on Carnival Sunday Night. His hugely popular "Trini" joins the growing list of patriotic songs affectionately referred to as unofficial national anthems of Trinidad and Tobago, but its popularity was not without controversy. The melody of this song is built around a heavy sample of Ed Watson's 1979 hit "You Gotta Give Away" sung by Singing Dianne. Soon after its release a chorus of dissenting voices was loud in their condemnation of what in their view was a blatant case of copyright infringement. Ed Watson himself confirmed that the music was used without his permission; he instructed the Copyright Organisation of Trinidad and Tobago (COTT) to step in on his behalf and after some to-ing and fro-ing an eventual settlement was agreed upon. "Trini" was produced by the New York-based Art and Life Studios.

Like Benaji, Blaxx was also a finalist in the Young Kings Calypso Monarch Competition, he sang "We Not Racial". He was also a semifinalist in the National Calypso Monarch Competition where he sang "Good Time".

After her third-place finish in the 2004 soca monarch finals Destra bowed out of competition. She returned in 2011, lured by the government-sponsored TT$2,000,000 purse for the Power Soca winner. She made it to both the Power and Groovy finals. The Groovy category was introduced in 2005 making her 2011 performance on Fantastic Friday her first experience on the Groovy Soca Monarch stage. Similarly, Denise Belfon who last competed in 2007 was back among the combatants, but for the first time in the Groovy segment of Fantastic Friday's programme.

Veteran calypsonian All Rounder is the oldest competitor to have ever graced the stage on Fantastic Friday. At age 71 and with a singing career which began in 1967, not many among this generation of soca lovers were even aware of his existence. His selection as a semifinalist was a surprise even to those who knew of him, but his performance at that semifinal round at the Arima Velodrome won him legions of new fans. With an infectious tune, comical lyrics and accompanying antics he demonstrated his "Body Wine" ably assisted by three sexily clad young ladies. His daughters, Lady Wonder and Shirlane Hendrickson, seasoned calypsonians themselves, provided background vocals as they do for all his performances. Shirlane was herself a Soca Monarch finalist in both 1999 and 2000. All Rounder proved undoubtedly that he was as deserving of his inclusion among the semifinalists as any of his much younger and more popular competitors.

By the time the finals rolled around "Body Wine" had received heavy rotation on the soca stations and was even being played in the carnival parties. On Fantastic Friday the veteran calypsonian kicked it up a notch with an age defying performance which at times could be described as risqué. Sporting a blonde mohawk-styled hairpiece, he was accompanied on stage this time by six sexily clad, wining young ladies and his two background-singing daughters who, on this occasion, also played active roles in the spicy stage antics.

All Rounder is no newcomer to the soca arena though; he was a finalist in 1993 and 1994 when the competition was just the National Soca Monarch Competition, limited to Trinidad and Tobago artistes and others residing there.

Ras Star gained automatic entry into the finals having won the 2011 Synergy Soca Star Competition.

2012

Date: Friday 17th February
Venue: National Stadium, Woodbrook, Trinidad & Tobago

Order of Appearance

	Artiste	Country
1	JW and Blaze	Trinidad and Tobago
2	Shal Marshall	Trinidad and Tobago
3	Destra	Trinidad and Tobago
4	Super Jigga TC	Trinidad and Tobago
5	Chucky	Trinidad and Tobago
6	Nadia Batson	Trinidad and Tobago
7	Erphaan Alves	Trinidad and Tobago
8	Blaxx	Trinidad and Tobago
9	Patrice Roberts	Trinidad and Tobago
10	KI	Trinidad and Tobago
11	Benjai	Trinidad and Tobago
12	Machel Montano	Trinidad and Tobago
13	Kees	Trinidad and Tobago
14	Kerwin Du Bois	Trinidad and Tobago

Results

Place	Artiste	Song
1	Machel Montano	Mr. Fete
2	Kerwin Du Bois	Bacchanalist
3	Benjai	People's Champion
4	Nadia Batson	No Pressure/Shiver
5	Kees	Stress Away
NOT DISCLOSED	Erphaan Alves	In Your Eyes
NOT DISCLOSED	JW and Blaze	We Time
NOT DISCLOSED	Shal Marshall	Trouble
NOT DISCLOSED	Destra	Baddist

Place	Artiste	Song
NOT DISCLOSED	Super Jigga TC	Action
	Chucky	Touch It
	Blaxx	Sound The Horn
	Patrice Roberts	I Am Soca
	KI	Single Forever

Before the draw for positions began, host Marc Anthony invited the defending monarchs in each category to either select what position they wished to perform in or be the first to draw. They also had the option to stop the draw at any point and select a number from the receptacle containing the numbers.

Dieffenthaller was not present for the draw and his manager, Simon Baptiste opted to be the first to pull a number. Defending Power Soca Monarch Machel Montano initially said to let it ride, but when Iwer George pulled position seven Montano stopped the draw and went to pull a number getting position nine.
[Express 14 February 2012]

Although Kerwin Du Bois fell just short of the mark in 2012, placing second behind Machel Montano, his song Bacchanalist was a huge crowd favourite throughout the carnival season. Like several other artistes Du Bois also entered the Power Soca Monarch Competition. He made it to the semifinal round, but opted out in order to concentrate on his Groovy performance:

At the performing position draw yesterday for the semi-final stage of the Digicel International Soca Monarch and Play Whe Groovy Soca Monarch at Carib Brewery, Champs Fleur, Dubois [sic] drew only for the Groovy Soca Monarch. When asked about it later he said, "I decided the best thing to do was to pull out of the Power Soca competition, and focus on just one thing. I do not want to burn out my energy when my heart and mind not into it".
[Newsday 26 January 2012]

"Make Room" would have been his selection for the Power Soca category.

On Saturday 10th March 2012, three weeks after his Groovy Soca Monarch performance Du Bois tied the knot with Shelly Edwards, his girlfriend of eight years in a beach wedding in Negril, Jamaica.

Kerwin Du Bois and Shelly Edwards Exchange Wedding Vows
Photo Courtesy Machel Montano

One week later on Saturday 17th March, after an eleven-year courtship, 2011 Groovy Soca Monarch, Kees Dieffenthaller, said his I "do's" to Terri Leigh Bovell. The nuptials took place in a small Catholic church in Patience Hill, Tobago.

Erphaan Alves was one of five finalists selected for both Power and Groovy categories in 2012. At twenty years old he was the youngest contestant to take the stage on Fantastic Friday. Alves is a prolific writer with quite an impressive list of artistes including Machel Montano, Kees Dieffehthaller, Patrice Roberts and Swappi among many others who have recorded songs penned by him.

One week prior to KI's Groovy Soca Monarch performance he copped the 2012 Chutney Soca Monarch Competition with his megahit "Single Forever". At age 26 he became the youngest Chutney Soca Monarch, walking away one million dollars richer for his efforts. KI was at the time one of the lead singers of the band JMC 3Veni. He is now the leader of the band which has been renamed KI And The Band. He repeated his Chutney Soca Monarch win in 2014, once again beating Rikki Jai into second place. The winning purse on that occasion was two million dollars; his winning song in 2014 was "Runaway". He won the Chutney Soca Monarch title once more in 2016 with "Same Gyal Twice", but would only make it as far as the semifinal round of the International Soca Monarch Competition. His Chutney Soca Monarch prize was one million dollars.

Destra was a guest artiste at the Chutney Soca Monarch Finals, she opened the show which was held at the Queen's Park Oval for the first time in the competition's history. She also accompanied Rikki Jai, the defending Chutney Soca Monarch, during his performance.

Blaxx was a contestant in the 2012 Young Kings Calypso Monarch Competition. He placed 12th among a field of eighteen singing "Sound The Horn".

On August 25th 2012 Mr. Chucky was crowned Trinidad and Tobago's 50th Anniversary of Independence Calypso Monarch (see page 79).

2013

Date: Friday 8th February
Venue: National Stadium, Woodbrook, Trinidad & Tobago

Order of Appearance

	Artiste	Country
1	Drupatee Ramgonai	Trinidad and Tobago
2	Nadia Batson	Trinidad and Tobago
3	Denise Belfon	Trinidad and Tobago
4	Ravi B	Trinidad and Tobago
5	Benjai	Trinidad and Tobago
6	Farmer Nappy	Trinidad and Tobago
7	Destra	Trinidad and Tobago
8	Patrice Roberts	Trinidad and Tobago
9	Machel Montano	Trinidad and Tobago
10	Iwer	Trinidad and Tobago
11	Blaxx	Trinidad and Tobago

Results

Place	Artiste	Song
1	Machel Montano	The Fog
2	Iwer	Bubble
3	Blaxx	Nah Get Away
4	Ravi B	Prescription
NOT DISCLOSED	Destra	Call My Name
NOT DISCLOSED	Benjai	Feter
NOT DISCLOSED	Nadia Batson	Manager
NOT DISCLOSED	Denise Belfon	Wining Queen
NOT DISCLOSED	Farmer Nappy	Stranger
NOT DISCLOSED	Patrice Roberts	A Little Wine
NOT DISCLOSED	Drupatee Ramgonai	Indian Gyal

Machel Montano's successful defense of the Groovy Soca Monarch title in 2013 established him as the first and only artiste in the short history of this competition to do so. Machel scored consecutive double victories (Power and Groovy Soca Monarch) in 2012 and 2013.

2014

Date: Friday 28th February
Venue: National Stadium, Woodbrook, Trinidad & Tobago

Order of Appearance

	Artiste	Country
1	Ravi B	Trinidad and Tobago
2	Mr. Famous	Trinidad and Tobago
3	Erphaan Alves	Trinidad and Tobago
4	Skinny Fabulous	St. Vincent and The Grenadines
5	Denise Belfon	Trinidad and Tobago
6	Biggie Irie	Barbados
7	Destra	Trinidad and Tobago
8	Tallpree	Grenada
9	Farmer Nappy	Trinidad and Tobago
10	Cassi	Trinidad and Tobago
11	Kerwin Du Bois	Trinidad and Tobago
12	Machel Montano	Trinidad and Tobago

Results

Place	Artiste	Song
1	Kerwin Du Bois	Too Real
2	Machel Montano	Happiest Man Alive
3	Farmer Nappy	Big People Party
4	Destra	First Time
NOT DISCLOSED	Erphaan Alves	Contagious
NOT DISCLOSED	Biggie Irie	Need A Rhythm
NOT DISCLOSED	Cassi	Man In Yuh House
NOT DISCLOSED	Tallpree	Jab Nation
NOT DISCLOSED	Denise Belfon	Chuku Chuku
NOT DISCLOSED	Ravi B	Bread
NOT DISCLOSED	Mr. Famous	Play More Local
NOT DISCLOSED	Skinny Fabulous	Behaving The Worst

A little known fact about Kerwin Du Bois is that he was twice a finalist in the Trinidad and Tobago National Calypso Monarch Competition. In 1996 he placed 3rd among a field of twelve singing "We Build This City" and "The Right And The Wrong". In 1997 he placed 5th, this time in a field of eleven; he sang "No Shade" and "Be Responsible". On both occasions Du Bois beat some of the biggest names in calypso. He was attached to the Kaiso House calypso tent during those respective carnival seasons.

National Calypso Monarch Finals

1996

1st Cro Cro; **2nd** Brother Marvin; **3rd Kerwin Du Bois**; **4th** Tigress; **5th** Sugar Aloes; **6th** Chalkdust; **7th** Delamo; **8th** Protector; **9th** Ella Andall; **10th** Black Stalin; **11th** Crazy; **12th** Luta.

1997

1st Gypsy; **2nd** Cro Cro; **3rd** Watchman; **4th** Black Stalin; **5th Kerwin Du Bois**; **6th** Kurt Allen; **7th** Sugar Aloes [Tie]; **7th** Ronnie McIntosh [Tie]; **9th** Tigress; **10th** GB; **11th** Ella Andall.

Kerwin Du Bois was also a Junior Calypso Monarch, having captured that title in 1992 as a student of Tranquility Government Secondary School. As a four-time finalist (1991 to 1994) he made quite a name for himself:

1991:   3rd place: "Street Culture"

1992:   1st Place: "Thing We Leave Behind"

1993:   2nd Place: "Maxi Dub"

1994:   10th Place: "Dem St. Clair Boys"

The Junior Calypso and Soca Monarch Competitions continue to be incubators of sorts for future stars of both genres in Trinidad and Tobago. Stars such as Machel Montano, Ghetto Flex, Natasha Wilson, Destra Garcia, Kurt Allen, Patrice Roberts and an extensive list of others have all graduated from these competitions.

2015

Date: Friday 13th February
Venue: National Stadium, Woodbrook, Trinidad & Tobago

Order of Appearance

	Artiste	Country
1	5 Star Akil	Trinidad and Tobago
2	Chow Chow	Trinidad and Tobago
3	Erphaan Alves	Trinidad and Tobago
4	Chucky	Trinidad and Tobago
5	Blaxx	Trinidad and Tobago
6	Skinny Fabulous	St. Vincent and The Grenadines
7	Destra	Trinidad and Tobago
8	Nadia Batson	Trinidad and Tobago
9	Farmer Nappy	Trinidad and Tobago
10	Ricardo Drue	Antigua and Barbuda / Trinidad and Tobago
11	Benjai	Trinidad and Tobago
12	Lyrikal	Trinidad and Tobago
13	Leadpipe and Saddis	Barbados
14	Fadda Fox	Barbados
15	Olatunji Yearwood	Trinidad and Tobago

Results

Place	Artiste	Song
1	Olatunji Yearwood	Ola
2	Farmer Nappy	My House
3	Ricardo Drue	Vagabond
4	Destra	Lucy
NOT DISCLOSED	Erphaan Alves	Bumper Like Rain
	Leadpipe and Saddis	Ah Feeling
	Fadda Fox	Duckin
	Benjai	Phenomenal

Place	Artiste	Song
NOT DISCLOSED	Chow Chow	Saga Boy
	5 Star Akil	Noise
	Lyrikal	Cloud 9
	Blaxx	Place In Life
	Nadia Batson	Cooler Party
	Chucky	Doh Take It On
	Skinny Fabulous	Going Off

The Prizes: 1st - $1,000,000; **2nd** - $400,000; **3rd** - $250,000; **4th** - $175,000; **5th to 15th** - $150,000

Chucky, straddling both the soca and calypso genres, holds the distinction of being Trinidad and Tobago's 50th Anniversary of Independence Calypso Monarch (winning that title on August 25th 2012), and two-time National Calypso Monarch (2014, 2015). Another artiste who can hold his own in both genres is Erphaan Alves who made his debut at the Kaiso Karavan Calypso Tent in 2014. Both Chucky and Erphaan Alves are graduates of the Junior Calypso Monarch Competition; so are Destra and Olatunji Yearwood.

The 2015 Breakout Artiste of the Year was Sekon Sta; his big song for the season was "The Best".

A new wild card draw was added to the competition to allow one of the four highest scoring non-qualifying semifinalists a chance at being selected for the finals on Fantastic Friday. This selection is based solely on votes texted in by customers of mobile phone network provider, Digicel, the sponsor of the Groovy Soca Monarch Competition. In contention for that final spot were Patrice Roberts, Ravi B, Sekon Sta and 5 Star Akil. The votes went in favour of 5 Star Akil.

After years of modest returns as a soca artiste in the Trinidad and Tobago market the elements fell in perfect alignment for Ricardo Drue with the release of his breakaway hit "Vagabond". The turn of the tide started for him when he won the Jumpy Soca Monarch title in his native Antigua & Barbuda during the carnival celebrations there in August 2014. His winning song was "Hide And Seek" while his performance of "Vagabond" earned him third place in the Groovy category. Notwithstanding his third place showing in both Antigua and Barbuda and at the 2015 International Soca Monarch Competition in Trinidad and Tobago, "Vagabond" was the song which propelled him to star status internationally. At the 12th Annual International Soca & Chutney Awards in September 2015 in Queens, New York, USA he walked away with the Best Video of the Year award for "Vagabond". In November at the COTT Music Awards in Trinidad and Tobago he won the People's Choice Breakout Artiste of the Year Award.

Drue successfully defended his Jumpy Soca title in Antigua and Barbuda in 2015 and finished second in the Groovy competition which was one better than he did in 2014. He sang "W.A.R." to win the Jumpy title; "Professional" was his Groovy song. Drue was born in Antigua, but moved to Trinidad and Tobago at the age of 4 where he spent most of his formative years. In his late teens he moved to Florida, USA where he is currently based.

In 2015, as was the case in 2012, Blaxx was selected as a finalist in both the power and groovy soca finals. He was also among the combatants in the 2015 Young Kings Calypso Competition at the Queen's Park Savannah on February 2. He placed 9th singing "Place in Life".

Ricardo Drue
Courtesy Ricardo Drue

Although he may not have known it at the time Ola's fantastic win on the Groovy Soca Monarch stage brought an end to the eleven year run of this aspect of the International Soca Monarch Competition. In November 2015 Caribbean Prestige Foundation For The Performing Arts launched what would be a major overhaul of the competition. Most notably was the move away from the two-category format; no longer would the artistes be pooled into "Power" and "Groovy" groupings.

> The Power and Groovy categories have been dropped from next year's Soca Monarch Competition, which will now be a straight Soca Show, according to Peter Scoon, Chairman of Caribbean Prestige Foundation [sic], organisers of the show. Scoon said there will be no live broadcast of the finals of Soca Monarch, no live streaming, or pay-per-view broadcast and the results will not be announced at the end of the show.
> **[Newsday 5 November 2015]**

> Scoon ... announced the scrapping of the Groovy and Power soca categories with competition in a single category. This would see a return to the original format which was changed in 2005 with the introduction of the Groovy soca category.
> **[Trinidad Guardian 5 November 2015]**

The Power Soca Finals
2007 - 2015

International Power Soca Monarch Competition 2007

Date: Friday, 16th February
Venue: National Stadium, Woodbrook, Trinidad & Tobago

Order of Appearance

	Artiste	Country
1	Dawg E. Slaughter	Trinidad and Tobago
2	Fay Ann Lyons-Alvarez	Trinidad and Tobago
3	Patrice Roberts	Trinidad and Tobago
4	Barry Chandler	Barbados
5	Nadia Batson Featuring Kees	Trinidad and Tobago
6	Iwer George	Trinidad and Tobago
7	Blaze and JW	Trinidad and Tobago
8	Shurwayne Winchester	Trinidad and Tobago
9	Blaxx	Trinidad and Tobago
10	Minmi	Japan
11	Saucy Wow and Spontaneous	Trinidad and Tobago/Grenada
12	Olatunji Yearwood	Trinidad and Tobago

Results

Place	Artiste	Song
1	Iwer George	Fete After Fete
2	Nadia Batson featuring Kees	My Land
3	Shurwayne Winchester	Open The Gates
4	Patrice Roberts	Light It Up
5	Blaze and JW	Eat Ah Food
6	Blaxx	Dutty
7	Olatunji Yearwood	Get Wild
8	Fay Ann Lyons-Alvarez	Make A Stage
9	Barry Chandler	Flames
10	Dawg E. Slaughter	Spread The Love
11	Saucy Wow featuring Spontaneous	Bicycle Wine
12	Minmi	Sha Na Na

Barry Chandler's "Flames" was written by Nadia Batson. This tune was Barbados' 2006 Crop Over road march. Nadia also wrote "Dutty" for Blaxx. Her prolific writing skills earned her the Copyright Organization of Trinidad and Tobago's 2006 songwriter of the year award.

In 2007 Nadia was a finalist at both the Power and Groovy Soca Monarch Competitions. At the Groovy final she sang "Caribbean Girl" and placed 3rd behind Barbadian Biggie Irie and Chucky. Biggie Irie, with this win, became the first non-Trinbagonian monarch (Groovy or Power) in the history of the competition; he sang "We Nah Going Home."

2008

Date: Friday, 1st February
Venue: Queen's Park Oval, St. Clair, Trinidad & Tobago

Order of Appearance

	Artiste	Country
1	Nnika	Grenada
2	Ricky T	St. Lucia
3	Luni Spark & Electrify	Grenada
4	Shurwayne Winchester	Trinidad and Tobago
5	Nadia Batson	Trinidad and Tobago
6	Iwer George	Trinidad and Tobago
7	Bunji Garlin	Trinidad and Tobago
8	Fay Ann Lyons-Alvarez	Trinidad and Tobago
9	Problem Child	St. Vincent & The Grenadines
10	Blaxx	Trinidad and Tobago
11	Pelf	Trinidad and Tobago

Results

Place	Artiste	Song
1	Bunji Garlin	Fiery
2	Iwer George	Over Yuh Head
3	Fay Ann Lyons-Alvarez	Get On
4	Nadia Batson	My Posse
5	Shurwayne Winchester	Whole Day
6	Blaxx	Breathless
7	Ricky T	Pressure Boom
8	Problem Child	Party Animal
9	Nnika [Tie]	Mas
9	Pelf [Tie]	Bumper
11	Luni Spark & Electrify	High

The husband and wife team of Bunji Garlin and Fay Ann Lyons-Alvarez left their mark on Carnival 2008. After a one-year hiatus Bunji made a triumphant return to the Soca Monarch Competition albeit amid calls for the disqualification of his song. "Fiery" as performed by Bunji is a remake of an old classic by calypso legend the late Maestro. Some felt Bunji shouldn't have been allowed to compete with this song, but a strong endorsement came from the chairman of the competition's governing body:

> Caribbean Prestige Foundation For The Performing Arts chairman, William Munro … said the artiste's remake of the late Maestro's hit is a valid submission. Munro asserted that there was "unnecessary controversy" against Garlin's song because of its similarities to the Maestro's composition. "Some artistes are saying that the song should not be in the International Soca Monarch but I am saying any artiste could sing any song they want." He added that once the artiste enters the song into the competition and is given the nod by the judges to compete, there should be no controversy over the artiste's choice. He explained the rules were changed to accommodate adapted versions of songs years ago when chutney star, Sonny Mann entered the 1996 competition with his 1995 song, "Lotay La." Munro added that Garlin's rendition of Maestro's classic shows his creativity and ability as a singer. **[Newsday 24 January 2008]**

A huge blow-up of a newspaper article announcing Maestro's untimely passing was one of the props Bunji used. Nearing the end of his performance he invited two of the late singer's relatives to the stage and made the following announcement as they danced to the music:

"Ladies and gentlemen of Trinidad and Tobago, who ever win the crown tonight win the crown, I have a more important mission ahead of me. Music like this must never stay hidden in the archives in Trinidad and Tobago again. This man here is the one called Scientist, is the cousin of Maestro. This one is Christian, is the nephew of Maestro; they came here tonight to show that they gave approval of me taking the things and doing it the right way."

Getting back into the song, Bunji turned to the blown-up newspaper article, which also contains a photo of Maestro, and sang a new verse, specially written for the occasion:

> *While you are sleeping*
> *Lying down in your grave*
> *Your legacy we will save*
> *While the crowd jump up and wave*
> *We hold you in the highest esteem*
> *They give you the keys to the city*
> *And they give you Trinity Cross*
> *They could give you the whole of Trinidad,*
> *but you still is a boss*
> *I know if you was here alive*
> *You woulda hug up here with your wife*
> *You woulda tell dem Bunji Garlin give dem lyrics*
> *and cut dem like knife*

Fay Ann's third place finish was met with loud disapproval from her fans--Bunji included--who felt she had performed well enough to earn either first or second place. By the end of carnival, though, "Get On" had proven to be the resounding favourite on the road, bringing her the Road March crown, her second. With these two victories (Soca Monarch and Road March) they became the first married couple, to have each won a major competition in the same carnival season.

Carnival 2008 also saw Bunji Garlin's debut at a calypso tent; he was the headline act at Kaiso House for the "Youth Vibes" segment of their programme. He was ably supported on stage by Fay-Ann.

Ricky T's "Pressure Boom" brought him his second consecutive St. Lucia Road March victory. He was joint winner in 2006, his song "Container" tying with Vertex Band's "My Pressure Up".

Problem Child took St. Vincent & The Grenadines' 2007 Road March title with the hugely popular "Party Animal". He scored his second road victory in 2009 with "Mad House".

Nnika won Best Female Vocalist at the 2007 International Soca Awards for her single "Don't Let Me Go".

2009

Date: Friday, 20th February
Venue: National Stadium, Woodbrook, Trinidad & Tobago

Order of Appearance

	Artiste	Country
1	Shurwayne Winchester	Trinidad and Tobago
2	Blaxx	Trinidad and Tobago
3	Patrice Roberts	Trinidad and Tobago
4	Khiomal	Barbados
5	Skinny Fabulous	St. Vincent and The Grenadines
6	Berbice	Grenada
7	Luni Spark & Electrify	Grenada
8	Fay Ann Lyons-Alvarez	Trinidad and Tobago
9	Ricky T	St. Lucia
10	Iwer George	Trinidad and Tobago
11	Bunji Garlin	Trinidad and Tobago
12	Claudette Peters	Antigua and Barbuda

Results

Place	Artiste	Song
1	Fay Ann Lyons-Alvarez	Meet Super Blue
2	Bunji Garlin [Tie]	Clear De Road
2	Iwer George [Tie]	Ready
4	Blaxx	Tusty
5	Skinny Fabulous	Head Bad (On The Spot)
6	Shurwayne Winchester	U Energy
7	Patrice Roberts	Sway D Mas
8	Berbice	Traffic
9	Luni Spark & Electrify	Clear De Way
10	Khiomal	Unleash The Beast
11	Claudette Peters	Bring It On
12	Ricky T	Wheel & Come Again

Performing just one week prior to having her first child Fay Ann Lyons-Alvarez took no prisoners in what has been, without question, her most successful carnival season thus far. In addition to the International Power Soca Monarch win she also copped the Groovy Soca Monarch title and the People's Choice prize on Fantastic Friday. On Ash Wednesday she was adjudged the 2009 Road March winner, successfully defending that title with "Meet Superblue". This song is a tribute to her father who holds the record for soca monarch wins; he is a seven-time soca monarch champion and has won nine Road March titles. He appeared on the soca monarch stage during her performance of the song. Fay Ann became the first female International Power Soca Monarch with this win. Her husband, Bunji Garlin, who she dethroned, stated during his performance that he was in the competition "just to have fun and to push Iwer out of second place, because we done know who come first." This led to a general feeling that he toned down his performance in support of his wife.

Fay Ann became the first female artiste to win both the Power and Groovy Soca titles in the same year. More impressively she also became the first artiste, male or female, to win the Power Soca, Groovy Soca, People's Choice and Road March titles in the same year. She gave birth to the couple's first, and to date, only child, a girl, on February 28th.

A new feature introduced to the International Soca Monarch Competition in 2009 was the seeding of the reigning power soca monarchs from the other Caribbean territories, allowing them automatic entry to the finals on Fantastic Friday. Skinny Fabulous, Ricky T, Claudette Peters, Khiomal and Luni Spark & Electrify were the first of the regional winners who took this route. That arrangement was, however, discontinued after the 2012 final.

"Head Bad (On The Spot)" was Skinny Fabulous' winning song at the 2008 St. Vincent & The Grenadines Soca Monarch Competition. In 2009 he received his country's Entertainer of the Year Award, took the first runner up spot in the Organization of Eastern Caribbean States (OECS) Soca Monarch Competition, and was adjudged Best New Male Artiste at the International Soca Music Awards. He also successfully defended his SVG Soca Monarch title with "Beast Let Go".

Ricky T won St. Lucia's Power Soca Monarch Competition in 2008 singing "Wheel And Come Again" which also brought him his third consecutive road march title. He successfully defended both titles in 2009 with "Like a Jumbie".

Claudette Peters has the distinction of being Antigua & Barbuda's most successful Party Monarch in the history of the competition. She is a four-time Jumpy Monarch, achieving the beaver trick from 2005 to 2008, and a five-time Groovy Monarch with titles in 2007, 2008, 2010, 2011 and 2015. She reigned supreme with double victories (Groovy and Jumpy Monarch titles) in 2007 and 2008. Peters was her country's first female monarch in 2005 and first Groovy Monarch in 2007. In 2006 she received the Best New Female Soca Artiste Award for her song "All I Know" at the International Soca Awards held in Queens, New York. Over the years she has chalked up quite an impressive list of accolades which are too many to mention in this space, but suffice it to say that she has etched her name indelibly in the annals of Antigua and Barbuda's soca lore.

Khiomal is a former Barbados Junior Calypso Monarch (1998). He received the award for Male Entertainer of the Year at the 2009 Barbados Music Awards.

Luni Spark & Electrify are sons of Grenada's first female calypso monarch, Lady Cinty. They became the first duo to win Grenada's Soca Monarch Competition in 2007 and successfully defended that title in 2008. They have made it to the Grenada finals on several other occasions.

Berbice, who was not among the finalists at the Grenada Soca Monarch Competition, battled his way through each round of the International Soca Monarch Competition on his way to the final on Fantastic Friday.

2010

Date: Friday, 12th February
Venue: Queen's Park Oval, St. Clair, Trinidad & Tobago

Order of Appearance

	Artiste	Country
1	Daddy Chess	Dominica
2	Tian Winter	Antigua and Barbuda
3	Super Jigga TC	Trinidad and Tobago
4	Shal Marshall & Screws	Trinidad and Tobago
5	Skinny Fabulous	St. Vincent and The Grenadines
6	Mr. Killa	Grenada
7	Tallpree	Grenada
8	Farmer Nappy	Trinidad and Tobago
9	Fay Ann Lyons-Alvarez	Trinidad and Tobago
10	JW & Blaze	Trinidad and Tobago
11	Blaxx	Trinidad and Tobago
12	KMC & Ronnie McIntosh	Trinidad and Tobago

Results

Place	Artiste	Song
1	JW & Blaze	Palance
2	Fay Ann Lyons-Alvarez	True Lies
3	Shal Marshall & Screws	Police
4	Tallpree	Wicked Jab
NOT DISCLOSED	Blaxx	Zombie
NOT DISCLOSED	Skinny Fabulous	Beast Let Go
NOT DISCLOSED	KMC & Ronnie McIntosh	While You Can
NOT DISCLOSED	Farmer Nappy	I Pay For This
NOT DISCLOSED	Mr. Killa	Swing It Away
NOT DISCLOSED	Daddy Chess	Read Or Not
NOT DISCLOSED	Tian Winter	Soca Rebels
NOT DISCLOSED	Super Jigga TC	The Template

Text voting was introduced to the Soca Monarch Competition as part of the adjudication process, allowing local, regional and North American fans to play an active role in deciding who wins the respective titles. Initially, votes texted in by the fans accounted for 35 percent of the artiste's final score while points awarded by the official judges accounted for 65 percent. This was adjusted in 2014 allowing the votes texted in by fans to account for just 5 percent of the final score.

JW & Blaze were the owners of the keys to carnival city in 2010. Prior to their resounding victories in both the Soca Monarch and Road March competitions, their mega song, "Palance," became an immediate hit very early in the carnival season, maintaining its popularity throughout. It enjoyed heavy rotation on the airwaves and was enormously popular on the party circuit. The song was written by Kernal Roberts who also wrote Tian Winter's "Soca Rebels" and, along with Screws (Tichard Barrington), co-wrote Shal Marshall and Screws' "Police".

Iwer George was scheduled to perform his 2010 hit "Party Hard" in position #10 but was a no-show on final night. Bunji Garlin opted out of the competition altogether to concentrate on assisting his wife (Fay Ann Lyons) in preparation and strategy for the defense of her Power and Groovy Soca Monarch titles. At the end of it all she fell just short of the mark, placing second in each of those competitions. Shurwayne Winchester was the 2010 Groovy Soca Monarch singing "Murdah".

Fay Ann Lyons was the lone female among the finalists in 2010, the second such occurrence in the history of the competition. The first was at the 1996 final when Denyse Plummer sang in position #4 among a field of 18. Her song was "Get On Bad" and it was the very first "International Soca Monarch Competition", rebranded to allow soca artistes from the wider Caribbean and beyond to participate. In the earlier years (1993 to 1995) the competition was labeled simply as the National Soca Monarch Competition, open strictly to Trinidad and Tobago nationals and others residing there. There is just one other instance to date when the females were almost shut out from the finals; the artiste was Patrice Roberts in 2016. She sang "Money Done" in position #9 among a field of 20. On a number of occasions there were just two female artistes among the finalists:

1997 Denyse Plummer and Melanie Hudson among a field of 25
2001 Destra and Denise Belfon among a field of 15
2012 Destra and Nadia Batson among a field of 12
2015 Patrice Roberts and Hot Mouth Granny among a field of 11

There has never been an instance of a full slate of male finalists.

Daddy Chess, Tian Winter, Skinny Fabulous and Mr. Killa were each granted automatic entry to the International Soca Monarch Finals by virtue of having captured the Soca Monarch title in their respective countries. Former Grenadian Soca Monarch, Tallpree, made it to the finals on his own strength, battling through each round of the competition.

In 2011 Daddy Chess achieved a hat trick of wins at the Dominica Soca Monarch Finals. He scored his first victory in 2008 when he sang "That's The Way We Like It". He repeated in 2009 with "Ready Or Not" and in 2011 with "Shameless". There was no competition in 2010. Daddy Chess is also the 2001 Dominica Calypso Monarch and 2008 Road March winner (2008). The Soca Monarch Competition in Dominica has been discontinued, its last staging being the 2011 edition. A new Bouyon Monarch Competition is expected to replace it. Bouyon is a genre of music indigenous to Dominica; it is a blend of Dominica's traditional music and dance including belle, quadrill, jing ping, mazouk, and kadance.

Skinny Fabulous completed the Soca Monarch hat-trick in St. Vincent (2008 – 2010). In 2011 he placed second to Fireman who to date is an eight-time winner of that competition. Skinny Fabulous returned to winner's row in 2012, 2013 and 2015. He was also the Ragga Soca Monarch in 2015. In 2016 he opted out of competition.

Tian Winter won Antigua and Barbuda's 2009 Groovy and Jumpy Party (Soca) Monarch titles. He followed in the footsteps of Claudette Peters who accomplished the double in 2007 and 2008. In 2010, again finding themselves among the finalists in both categories, Peters copped the Groovy Monarch title and Winter took the Jumpy. To date they have maintained their supremacy over the Party Monarch scene in Antigua and Barbuda. Peters, though, stands tallest among them all with an unprecedented nine victories altogether including a beaver trick of wins (2005 – 2008). She was Antigua and Barbuda's first female monarch in 2005 and the country's first Groovy Monarch in 2007. Ricardo Drue who has also enjoyed a consistent run of success over the years has joined Claudette Peters and Tian Winter in the fight to hold on to that top spot. Tian Winter's hat-trick of "Groovy" wins (2012 – 2014) further underscores the trio's dominance.

Groovy	Jumpy
2011 1st Claudette Peters - "Work It" 2nd Tian Winter - "Crash" 3rd Jashan - "Wuck"	1st Hard Knoxx - "Kentucky" 2nd Tian Winter - "Soca Quake" 3rd Claudette Peters - "Work It"
2012 1st Tian Winter - "Cyah Fail Me" 2nd Claudette Peters - "Benna Sauce" 3rd Ricardo Drue - "Sugah"	1st Tian Winter – "Raving" 2nd Ricardo Drue – "Supaman" 3rd Natural Rampler "Countdown"
2013 1st Tian Winter – "Roaming" 2nd Set On – "Smile" 3rd Claudette Peters – "Belong To A Flag"	1st Ezzy – "Golden Cup" 2nd Tian Winter – "Aint Got No Time For That" 3rd Hard Knoxx – "Jam Jam"
2014 1st Tian Winter – "Cyah Miss It" 2nd Menace – "Fete" 3rd Ricardo Drue – "Vagabond"	1st Ricardo Drue – "Hide & Seek" 2nd Claudette Peters – "Fireworks" 3rd Ezzy – "Debel Riddim"
2015 1st Claudette Peters – "Nasty" 2nd Ricardo Drue – "Professional" 3rd Boasta – "Old Time Something"	1st Ricardo Drue – "W.A.R." 2nd Claudette Peters – "D'General" 3rd Tian Winter – "Voices Inside My Head"
2016 1st Ricardo Drue – "Stamp Your Name" 2nd Claudette Peters – "On My Behalf" 3rd Tian Winter – "Can't Explain"	1st Tian Winter – "In D Middle" 2nd Dennis Roberts – "Spartans" 3rd Claudette Peters – "Hungry"

Claudette Peters, Tian Winter and Ricardo Drue seem to have the formula for success at Antigua and Barbuda's Party Monarch Competition.

Mr. Killa was an International Soca Monarch finalist in 2005, placing 14th; he was then known as Baby Killa. He is a three-time (2004, 2006 and 2009) Grenada Soca Monarch. In 2006 he scored the double taking both the "Power" and "Groovy" titles. In 2009 "Swing It Away" earned him not only the Soca Monarch Title, but the Road March as well.

2011

Date: Friday, 4th March
Venue: National Stadium, Woodbrook, Trinidad & Tobago

Order of Appearance

	Artiste	Country
1	JW & Blaze	Trinidad and Tobago
2	Blood	Barbados
3	Skinny Fabulous	St. Vincent and The Grenadines
4	Michelle Xavier	Trinidad and Tobago
5	Shal Marshall	Trinidad and Tobago
6	Tallpree	Grenada
7	Iwer George	Trinidad and Tobago
8	Nadia Batson & Patrice Roberts	Trinidad and Tobago
9	Machel Montano	Trinidad and Tobago
10	Destra	Trinidad and Tobago
11	Ravi B.	Trinidad and Tobago
12	Bunji Garlin	Trinidad and Tobago
13	Tian Winter	Antigua and Barbuda
14	Fay Ann Lyons-Alvarez	Trinidad and Tobago

Results

Place	Artiste	Song
1	Machel Montano	Advantage
2	Iwer George	Come To Meh
3	Bunji Garlin	Hold A Burn
4	Fay Ann Lyons-Alvarez	Consider It Done
NOT DISCLOSED	JW & Blaze	Wild & Frisky
NOT DISCLOSED	Blood	Foot On Fire
NOT DISCLOSED	Skinny Fabulous	Charge Up
NOT DISCLOSED	Michelle Xavier	Fettin For Days

Place	Artiste	Song
NOT DISCLOSED	Shal Marshall	Doh Drag De Flag
	Nadia Batson & Patrice Roberts	We Not Leaving
	Tallpree	Lighters
	Destra	We Own It
	Tian Winter	Hurricane
	Ravi B.	Is Mas

Machel Montano and Destra were lured back into competition by what, to date, is the biggest purse in the history of the International Soca Monarch Competition. Living up to a campaign promise, the then newly elected (May 24th 2010) People's Partnership Government of Trinidad and Tobago sponsored the first prize of $2,000,000 TTD for four of the country's major carnival competitions; (Chutney Soca, National Panorama - Large Bands, National Calypso Monarch and the International Power Soca Monarch). Prior to his triumphant return Machel's best showing was his last in 1996 when he placed 3rd singing "Make A Borrow". Destra bowed out of competition after her third-place finish in 2004 with "Bonnie And Clyde". On her re-entry in 2011 she was a finalist in both the Power and Groovy Soca Monarch Competitions; it was her first foray into the Groovy Soca Monarch which was not an item on the carnival calendar of events until 2005.

Machel celebrated a second victory on Ash Wednesday when "Advantage" was declared the most popular tune on the road on Carnival Monday and Tuesday. This brought him his fourth Road March title. Credit goes to Kernal Roberts from whose pen this and countless other hit songs have come.

Tian Winter, Skinny Fabulous and Blood were the automatic entrants to the finals, having captured the Soca Monarch title in their respective countries. As he did in 2010, Tallpree battled through each round of the competition to earn his spot in the finals.

In 2010 Skinny Fabulous completed a hat trick of wins (2008 – 2010) at the St. Vincent & The Grenadines Soca Monarch Competition. "Charge Up" also earned him second place in the Road March battle there.

Blood won his first Barbados Tune-of-the-Crop (Road March) title with "Foot On Fire"

2012

Date: Friday, 17th February
Venue: National Stadium, Woodbrook, Trinidad & Tobago

Order of Appearance

	Artiste	Country
1	Mikey	Barbados
2	Fireman	St. Vincent and The Grenadines
3	Erphaan Alves	Trinidad and Tobago
4	Destra	Trinidad and Tobago
5	Nadia Batson	Trinidad and Tobago
6	Shurwayne Winchester	Trinidad and Tobago
7	Iwer George	Trinidad and Tobago
8	Blaxx	Trinidad and Tobago
9	Machel Montano	Trinidad and Tobago
10	Prophet Benjamin	Trinidad and Tobago
11	Hard Knoxx	Antigua and Barbuda
12	Swappi	Trinidad and Tobago

Results

Place	Artiste	Song
1	Machel Montano	Pump Yuh Flag
2	Iwer George	No Pain
3	Destra	Link Up
4	Prophet Benjamin [Tie]	Throw Wine
4	Blaxx [Tie]	Inside Ah Band/Inna Band
NOT DISCLOSED	Erphaan Alves	Terrible
NOT DISCLOSED	Hard Knoxx	Kentucky
NOT DISCLOSED	Mikey	Pavement Anticipation
NOT DISCLOSED	Fireman	Animal
NOT DISCLOSED	Nadia Batson	No Pressure
NOT DISCLOSED	Shurwayne Winchester	We Love
NOT DISCLOSED	Swappi	Bucket

Before the draw for positions began, host Marc Anthony invited the defending monarchs in each category to either select what position they wished to perform in or be the first to draw. They also had the option to stop the draw at any point and select a number from the receptacle containing the numbers.

Dieffenthaller was not present for the draw and his manager, Simon Baptiste opted to be the first to pull a number. Defending Power Soca Monarch Machel Montano initially said to let it ride, but when Iwer George pulled position seven Montano stopped the draw and went to pull a number getting position nine.
[Express 14 February 2012]

Machel Montano picked up from where he left off in 2011, successfully defending his Power Soca Monarch title on Fantastic Friday Night. He then claimed his fifth Road March title with "Pump Yuh Flag" which was played more than any other song at the various judging points throughout the country on Carnival Monday and Tuesday.

At a press conference…Montano said the song was originally to be called 'Pump Yuh Fist'…. Songwriter and producer Kernel [sic] Roberts admitted the song which he wrote came from an advertisement he was doing for a company, which rejected it. Montano said when they changed the name to 'Pump Yuh Flag' the song started to come together for them.
[Newsday 23 February 2012]

The Power category was billed as a clash between Montano and "Iwer" and it definitely played out that way, with both artistes getting the biggest crowd response on the night.
[Newsday 19 February 2012]

Machel also won his first Groovy Soca Monarch title with "Mr. Fete".

Husband and wife duo Bunji Garlin and Fay Ann Lyons, perennial soca monarch favourites, announced in 2012 that they would no longer be competing. To date they have maintained that stance.

"Kentucky" was a runaway hit for Hard Knoxx during Antigua and Barbuda's 2011 carnival season; it earned him both the Jumpy Soca Monarch and Road March titles that year. He along with Mikey and Fireman advanced to the International Soca Monarch Finals by virtue of an arrangement dating back to 2009 which allowed the reigning power soca monarchs from other Caribbean territories automatic selection as finalists on Fantastic Friday. That arrangement was discontinued after the 2012 final.

2013

Date: Friday 8th February
Venue: National Stadium, Woodbrook, Trinidad & Tobago

Order of Appearance

	Artiste	Country
1	Lil Bits	Trinidad and Tobago
2	Fya Empress	St. Vincent and the Grenadines
3	Tallpree	Grenada
4	Devon Matthews	Trinidad and Tobago
5	Shurwayne Winchester	Trinidad and Tobago
6	Benjai	Trinidad and Tobago
7	Destra	Trinidad and Tobago
8	JW & Blaze	Trinidad and Tobago
9	Machel Montano	Trinidad and Tobago
10	Swappi	Trinidad and Tobago
11	SuperBlue	Trinidad and Tobago

Results

Place	Artiste	Song
1	Machel Montano [Tie]	Float
1	SuperBlue [Tie]	Fantastic Friday
3	Benjai	Engoma
4	Destra	Carry On
NOT DISCLOSED	Lil Bits	Raise D Dust
NOT DISCLOSED	Fya Empress	Rum Please
NOT DISCLOSED	Devon Matthews	Start It Up
NOT DISCLOSED	Shurwayne Winchester	We Control The Road
NOT DISCLOSED	Tallpree	Muddy Jab
NOT DISCLOSED	JW & Blaze	Timing It
NOT DISCLOSED	Swappi	Cha-os

After more than a decade in obscurity Superblue made a phenomenally successful return to the International Soca Monarch Competition in 2013 with the hugely popular "Fantastic Friday". This song announces his triumphant return to the big stage on Fantastic Friday a.k.a. the International Soca Monarch Finals. Here are the first verse and chorus:

> Lord ah pray and ah pray
> For a day like today
> Bright and shinning
> Soca glory
> Everyone with a flag
> And a smile on they face
> Lordy dordy
> Of every creed and race, Lord
> Phenomenal, lovely atmosphere
> If the lord is our shepherd
> Who shall we fear
>
> Aye-ya-yaye, the party start
> Fantastic Friday
> Sincerely from your heart
> Thank God it's Friday
> I'm just here to say I love you
> Fantastic Friday
> A voice from out the blue
> Thank God it's Friday
> Friday, mash up the place
> Friday, in front they face
> Friday, red, white and black
> Friday, I'm back

"Fantastic Friday" was an immediate hit which became increasingly infectious as the season wore on. The frenzy and excitement created by this song took SuperBlue back into soca music's stratosphere where he resided before his extended slump. Very early in the carnival season, long before the soca monarch finals, the stage seemed to be set for a grand slam showdown between SuperBlue and defending champion Machel Montano. The prognosticators were correct and a massive crowd was on hand to witness the epic battle. At the end of it all a tie for first place was the result based on scores computed from points awarded by the judges and votes texted in by soca fans around the world. SuperBlue's last appearance prior to this was in 2002 when he placed 11th in a final night lineup of eighteen combatants; his song was "Peace Party". "Fantastic Friday" brought win number 7 for him, further extending his lead on all others who have won this competition; he was the first winner in 1993. With five Power Soca victories Machel Montano stands in second place among the all-time winners.

"Fantastic Friday" was played 511 times for masquerade bands at the adjudication points throughout the country on Carnival Monday and Tuesday, earning SuperBlue his 9th roadmarch title. This was the exclamation point on his 2013 carnival season. Not only did he set a new record for the number of times a tune was played in the Road March race, but he also scored the largest margin of victory in the history of the competition. In second place was Machel Montano's "Float" which was played 56 times.

As the dust settled on carnival 2013 elaborate plans were being put in place to pay tribute to SuperBlue leading up to and during the Point Fortin Borough Day Celebrations. He is a native of this southern city.

> The Point Fortin Borough Day celebrations this year will be all about SuperBlue.
>
> Sixteen solid days of activities to celebrate the 30th anniversary for Point Fortin becoming a borough, will kick off on April 19 at Victor Chin Kit Park and end on May 4 with Pan-on-the-Move, which this year will be rechristened Pan-For-Blue.
>
> The celebration usually attracts over 30,000 visitors, but Point Fortin Mayor Clyde Paul said yesterday: "Borough Day is expected to be big this year, because of the achievement of Austin 'SuperBlue' Lyons."
> Paul said the borough would give thanks for its icon, Superblue, who did them proud by winning the Road March and joint Soca Monarch titles in 2013.

He said after the statutory council meeting, he would proclaim Friday May 3, as SuperBlue Day.

He said: "A special thanksgiving service will also be held at the Town Hall in his honour," he said, "following which we will do the unveiling of a street sign, near where he was born in Point Fortin.

"That street, previously called Sylvester Street, will now be known as Austin Lyons Street. We will also turn the sod for a play park, near Point Fortin Area Hospital, which will also be named in his honour."

At its civic reception April 30, the actual day Point Fortin was made a borough, Super would be handed the keys to the borough, he added.
[Trinidad Guardian 28 February 2013]

Sylvester Street was actually renamed Austin Lyons Avenue.

Another big and unfolding story which kept tongues wagging throughout the 2013 carnival season was Machel Montano's legal woes resulting from an incident at the Zen nightclub in 2007.

> SOCA STAR Machel Montano was this morning found guilty of five criminal offences. Montano, the reigning Power Soca Monarch and Road March king, along with Kernel Roberts, the son of legendary Calypso icon Lord Kitchener, Joel "Zan" Feveck, a member of Montano HD Family, and Rodney "Benjai" LeBlanc, best known for his patriotic song, Trini, were all charged with a series of criminal offences arising out a fracas outside the Zen nightclub, in Port of Spain in April 2007.

After postponing her decision on two consecutive occasions, Magistrate Maureen Baboolal-Gafoor, presiding in the Port of Spain Magistrates Court, delivered her decision to a packed courtroom this morning. Montano was found guilty on four charges of assault against Gerard Borwin, Brandis Browne, Janelle Lee Chee and Russell Pollonais. Montano was also found guilty of using obscene language during the same incident. Roberts, the composer of several of Montano's hits, was also found guilty on two charges of assault while Benjai, who was charged with two offences of assault and Feveck, who was charged with a single offence of assault, were found not guilty. Magistrate Baboolal-Gafoor adjourned the matter to January 17, 2013, after hearing pleas of leniency from the attorneys representing the two men. She ordered that they remain free on bail pending her decision.

[Published online on 10th December, 2012]
http://www.trinidadexpress.com/news/BREAKING-NEWS---Machel-Montano-guilty-on-five-criminal-charges-182817341.html

The million dollar question was whether or not Machel should be sentenced to jail time or community service. With eyes on the January 17th sentencing date the bigger question then was whether or not he would be free to defend his Power and Groovy Soca Monarch titles and what would the carnival season be without his presence should he be sent to jail. The tension was eased when Magistrate Baboolal-Gafoor further adjourned sentencing to February 25th to allow for time to consider legal submissions made on January 16th by both the State and defence attorneys. There were no further delays.

SOCA STAR Machel Montano was yesterday spared a possible jail sentence after he was convicted of four assault charges and instead ordered to compensate the victims of the attack as well as pay fines to the court. In her ruling delivered shortly after 1 p.m., Magistrate Maureen Baboolal-Gafoor rejected a submission for Montano and songwriter Kernal Roberts, who was also convicted on two assault charges, to serve community service for the offences.

Baboolal-Gafoor's decision came almost six years after Montano's first court appearance. ...

The magistrate ordered Montano to pay compensation totalling $13,500 and fines totalling $13,700. Roberts was ordered to pay compensation totalling $11,000 and fines totalling $13,000.
[Express 26 February 2013]

By this time the carnival season was over and Machel was the recently crowned Groovy Soca Monarch and joint Power Soca Monarch, having successfully defended both titles.

Fya Empress didn't secure a place among the top three in the International Soca Monarch Finals but she entered the competition with quite an impressive string of victories under her belt. In January of 2012 she beat a field of 16 competitors in winning the National Women's Action Committee (NWAC) Calypso Queen title at the National Academy for the Performing Arts (NAPA) in Trinidad and Tobago. She followed that with the Tobago Calypso Queen title. In St. Vincent and the Grenadines later that year she was crowned Ragga Soca Monarch, Calypso Monarch and Roadmarch champion, and was second to Skinny Fabulous in the Soca Monarch Competition. Fya Empress is a Vincentian based in Tobago where she has also scored victories in the Calypso and Soca Monarch Competitions.

2014

Date: Friday, 28th February
Venue: National Stadium, Woodbrook, Trinidad & Tobago

Order of Appearance

	Artiste	Country
1	Ann-G	Japan
2	Snakey	Trinidad and Tobago
3	Nadia Batson	Trinidad and Tobago
4	Patrice Roberts	Trinidad and Tobago
5	SuperBlue	Trinidad and Tobago
6	Iwer	Trinidad and Tobago
7	Lyrikal	Trinidad and Tobago
8	Devon Matthews	Trinidad and Tobago
9	Destra	Trinidad and Tobago
10	Mr. Killa	Grenada
11	Machel Montano	Trinidad and Tobago

Results

Place	Artiste	Song
1	Machel Montano	Ministry Of Road
2	Destra [Tie]	Mash Up
2	Mr. Killa [Tie]	Rolly Polly
2	Iwer George [Tie]	Mama Oye
NOT DISCLOSED	Devon Matthews	Level It
NOT DISCLOSED	Patrice Roberts	Fetting Di Most
NOT DISCLOSED	Nadia Batson	Rated R
NOT DISCLOSED	Lyrikal	Lockdown
NOT DISCLOSED	Snakey	The Dhoti Song
NOT DISCLOSED	Ann-G	We Love Carnival
NOT DISCLOSED	SuperBlue	Carnival Yo Yo

After knocking on the door for some time Mr. Killa finally made the breakthrough in Trinidad and Tobago in 2014 with "Rolly Polly". This song which was an immediate favourite among soca lovers enjoyed heavy rotation on the local airwaves throughout the carnival season. In addition, no major fete or event was complete without a performance by the energetic and effervescent Grenadian artiste. He is a three-time (2004, 2006 and 2009) Grenada Soca Monarch.

In an effort to bring attention to emerging talent a new category labeled as The Breakout Artiste Of The Year was added to the International Soca Monarch Competition in 2014. The winner of this title is decided by a tally of votes sent in by fans. Mr. Killa emerged as the first title holder in this category edging out Erphaan Alves who was the only other artiste in contention.

Snakey enjoyed national popularity in 2014 with his breakout hit "The Dhoti Song" which took him to the finals of Chutney Soca Monarch Competition (February 15th) and the Young Kings Calypso Monarch Competition (February 17th) before hitting the International Power Soca Monarch Stage on Fantastic Friday (February 28th). He was also a National Calypso Monarch semi-finalist at Skinner Park (February 22) where he sang in position #1. Interestingly, on the same night he competed in the Young Kings Competition at The National Academy For The Performing Arts (NAPA) he also competed in the Extempo Calypso Competition at the Queen's Park Savannah. The "double play" was possible because the close proximity of both venues to each other allowed him the time to appear in position #7 in the Young Kings Competition and then at the Extempo contest where, in the first round, he performed in the last position at # 25. He may have been allowed a few extra minutes to get to the second venue, though, because he was scheduled to perform at # 24. In the Young Kings Calypso Monarch finals he placed third in a lineup of 22 contestants and made it as far as the second round of the Extempo Competition. He did not make the cut for the finals on February 27th.

2015

Date: Friday, 13th February
Venue: National Stadium, Woodbrook, Trinidad & Tobago

Order of Appearance

	Artiste	Country
1	Shurwayne Winchester	Trinidad and Tobago
2	Squeeze Head & Shal Marshall	Grenada/Trinidad and Tobago
3	KI	Trinidad and Tobago
4	Patrice Roberts	Trinidad and Tobago
5	Mr. Killa	Grenada
6	Granny	Trinidad and Tobago
7	Snakey	Trinidad and Tobago
8	Iwer	Trinidad and Tobago
9	Machel Montano	Trinidad and Tobago
10	Blaxx	Trinidad and Tobago
11	Kernal Roberts	Trinidad and Tobago

Results

Place	Artiste	Song
1	Machel Montano	Like Ah Boss
2	Iwer George	Play De People Mas
3	Granny	Go Granny
4	Shurwayne Winchester	Shake
NOT DISCLOSED	KI	Flags
NOT DISCLOSED	Blaxx	Maddest Crew
NOT DISCLOSED	Snakey	Cyar Rhyme
NOT DISCLOSED	Squeeze Head & Shal Marshall	Turbo Charge
NOT DISCLOSED	Kernal Roberts	Excitement
NOT DISCLOSED	Patrice Roberts	Trouble
NOT DISCLOSED	Mr. Killa	When We Reach

Blaxx took part in the Young Kings Calypso Monarch Competition at the Queen's Park Savannah on February 2nd; he placed 9th singing "Place in Life".

In 2015 the governing body of the Soca Monarch Competition, Caribbean Prestige Foundation For The Performing Arts, rescinded the rule which made it mandatory for the winner of each competition (Power and Groovy) to defend the title. This was soon followed by Kerwin DuBois' decision to opt out of defending his Groovy Soca Monarch Title. Machel Montano decided to give his fans one final blast before bowing out of the competition, successfully defending his Power Soca Monarch title on that Fantastic Friday night. For him it was his fifth consecutive victory.

> Montano said while he remains a source of support for all local artistes of all genres who are seeking advice and direction, he has firmly set his sights on his lifelong dream of winning a Grammy award and taking his music to mainstream international markets.
>
> "I want to make soca music now to touch the world. I believe we have something to offer and I believe now is the time. I believe we are being guided to do so and I want to follow this guidance." Montano said following his win on Friday…. "The whole Soca Monarch battle is no longer for me. I don't believe I have anything to battle anymore. I always compete with myself and right now, myself challenging me to win a Grammy".

[Sunday Express 15 February 2015]

The evolution continues for Machel, "Monk Monte" being his latest moniker to date.

> "Monk Monte is really the messenger of the monk philosophy and is a movement of new knowledge and that movement of new knowledge is flowing within me but it is a movement where I inspire people to learn things, to rediscover each other first of all and then different cultures….The word Monk is in keeping with my basic tradition to reinvent myself. Why do I reinvent myself [sic] because it is a natural phenomenon that happens in me, it is like molting, like shedding skin. Is like every three years I feel like I have to become higher". He revealed that his father's amiable personality was the inspiration behind the Monte part of his new name.

[Trinidad Guardian 6 February 2015]

International Soca Monarch Competition 2016

Date: Friday, 5th February
Venue: National Stadium, Woodbrook, Trinidad & Tobago

Order of Appearance

	Artiste	Country
1	Cloud 5	Grenada
2	M1 aka Menace	Trinidad and Tobago
3	Peter Ram	Barbados
4	Hypasounds	Barbados
5	Lyrikal	Trinidad and Tobago
6	Sekon Sta	Trinidad and Tobago
7	Preedy	Trinidad and Tobago
8	Shurwayne Winchester	Trinidad and Tobago
9	Patrice Roberts	Trinidad and Tobago
10	Pternsky	Trinidad and Tobago
11	Farmer Nappy	Trinidad and Tobago
12	5 Star Akil	Trinidad and Tobago
13	Teddyson John	St. Lucia
14	Shal Marshall	Trinidad and Tobago
15	Ricardo Drue	Antigua and Barbuda / Trinidad and Tobago
16	Third Bass	Trinidad and Tobago
17	Rikki Jai	Trinidad and Tobago
18	Blaxx	Trinidad and Tobago
19	Voice	Trinidad and Tobago
20	Olatunji Yearwood	Trinidad and Tobago

Results

Place	Artiste	Song
1	Voice	Cheers To Life
2	Preedy	Veteran
3	Patrice Roberts [Tie]	Money Done

Place	Artiste	Song
3	Blaxx [Tie]	Masters Of Mas
	Olatunji Yearwood	Oh Yey
	Rikki Jai	Leh We Fete
	Shurwayne Winchester	Truck Driver
	Shal Marshall	Party
NOT DISCLOSED	Peter Ram	All Ah We
	Cloud 5	No Behaviour
	Hypasounds	How She Like It
	Lyrikal	Freedom
	Third Bass	Bum Bum (If Yuh Stush Go In The Bush)
	Ricardo Drue	Bet
	Teddyson John	Allez
	5 Star Akil	Different Me
	Sekon Sta	Magic
	Farmer Nappy	Bambilambambilambilambam
	M1 aka Menace	Trouble (When The Sun Rise)
	Pternsky	Non Stop

In 2015 Soca Monarch's governing body, Caribbean Prestige Foundation For The Performing Arts, rescinded the rule which made it mandatory for the winner of the competition to defend the title. In 2016 another major shift away from what had become the norm was the decision to discontinue the dual Power/Groovy competition format which dates back to 2005 when Michelle Sylvester won the first Groovy Soca Monarch title (see page 1). This development reverts to the original competition structure which existed before the terms "power soca" and "groovy soca" were coined. The classification of the music according to beats per minute has been dropped and once again, as in the earlier years of the competition, there is an open forum. All entrants are drawn together at the preliminary round and the adjudication process takes the competition along its natural path to the grand showdown at the final round on Fantastic Friday.

The Soca Monarch Competition was added to calendar of carnival events in 1993 as a competition open exclusively to Trinidad and Tobago artistes and others residing there. First to perform on that inaugural night was calypsonian Revealer who sang "Once Yuh Popular". Superblue, who performed in position #23 among a field of 29 finalists, emerged as the world's first Soca Monarch, his winning song was "Bacchanal Time". Three years later, in 1996, the competition was rebranded as the International Soca Monarch Competition, open to singers of all nations. To date, however, the vast majority have come from Caribbean nations with just Minmi (2007) and Ann G (2014), both of Japan, and Celtic Invasion (2002) of the USA representing nations outside of the region.

The change in format in 2016 was but one component of a marketing strategy which included a few other elements:

> Organisers Caribbean Prestige Foundation [sic] … made several changes to the show's format, forgoing a live broadcast to create an edited package for delayed transmission yesterday evening. This meant results would be kept secret until the show's airing on local television yesterday and pay-per-view….
>
> Added to that, a last-minute advisory from CPF appeared on social media on Friday, warning patrons

against the posting of amateur footage and photos from the event on all social media platforms before today's date.

The notice further instructed that persons in violation of this rule could face prosecution.
[Sunday Express 7 February 2016]

There were mixed reactions to these changes from patrons and several artistes as well.

At 23 years old Voice became the youngest Soca Monarch to date. Bunji Garlin was 24 when he won in 2002. Conversely, Shadow was eight months short of his 60th birthday when he claimed victory in 2001. He is easily the oldest to have ever worn the Soca Monarch crown.

The 2016 Breakout Artiste of the Year was Jadel; her big song for the season was "All Of It". Salty was the other artiste in contention; his big song was "Girl Meets Brass". Although they both performed on the big stage on Fantastic Friday the winner would have already been decided based votes texted in by the public. From all indications Jadel's victory was the result of a well planned and executed campaign in the days and weeks leading up to the period open for public voting. Her prize was $100,000.

Another aspect of the Fantastic Friday experience which is decided on by public voting is the wildcard draw. When it was introduced in 2015 this vote opened the door to the finals for one of the four highest scoring Groovy Soca Monarch semi-finalists who didn't make the cut. Having moved away from the two-category format in 2016 the wildcard draw allowed for two open spots to the finals. The four artistes in contention were Kernal Roberts singing "Legacy", Peter Ram with 'All Ah We", M1 aka Menace with "Trouble (When The Sun Rise)", and Jaiga's "Anyway". The votes went in favour of Peter Ram and M1.

Patrice Roberts was the lone female finalist in 2016, the third such occurrence in the history of the Soca Monarch competition. Denise Plummer was the first in 1996 followed by Fay Ann Lyons in 2010 (see pages 31 and 32).

Rikki Jai is enjoying an illustrious career which straddles the soca, chutney soca, traditional chutney, and calypso genres. He was among the twenty-nine finalists at the inaugural Soca Monarch Competition in 1993. Twenty-three years later, in 2016, he made his sixth trip to the finals with "Leh We Fete". Of particular note, though, are the unprecedented seven Chutney Soca Monarch victories he has chalked up to date (1998, 1999, 2001, 2002, 2003, 2011 and 2015). He teamed up with the 2010 Chutney Soca Monarch, Ravi B, for the 2015 victory. Rikki Jai also took the 2015 Traditional Chutney Monarch title. In 2016 he placed 4th in the Chutney Soca Competition. Rikki Jai has also been quite prolific on the calypso circuit since his first foray into the genre late in 1988 when he recorded "Sumintra" for the 1989 carnival season. As a seasoned campaigner in 2001 he was crowned joint Young Kings Calypso Monarch with Bunji Garlin and was a 7th placed finalist in the National Calypso Monarch Competition.

Rikki Jai has also won the following titles:

1999	**National Chutney Monarch**
2000	**National Chutney Monarch**
2001	**South Calypso Monarch**
2001	**Unattached Calypso Monarch**
2005	**Chutney Mardi Gras Monarch**
2006	**Chutney Soca Monarch (New York)**
2012	**50th Anniversary Independence Chutney Soca Monarch**

Rikki Jai Performing at the 2016 International Soca Monarch Competition
Photo Courtesy Slam 100.5 FM

The Calypso Finals
2007 - 2016

National Calypso Monarch Competition
2007

Date: Sunday 18th February
Venue: Jean Pierre Complex, Woodbrook, Trinidad & Tobago

Order of Appearance

	Artiste	Given Name
1	Crazy	Edwin Ayoung
2	Devon Seale	Devon Seale
3	Heather Mac Intosh	Heather Mac Intosh
4	Sean Daniel	Sean Daniel
5	Valentino	Emrold Phillip
6	Maria Bhola	Maria Bhola
7	Black Sage	Phillip Murray
8	Shadow	Winston Bailey
9	Singing Sandra	Sandra Des Vignes-Millington
10	Mr. Caesar	Jervae Caesar
11	Skatie	Carlos James
12	Chalkdust	Dr. Hollis Liverpool
13	De Fosto	Winston Scarborough
14	Duane O'Connor	Duane O'Connor
15	Cro Cro	Weston Rawlins

Results

Place	Artiste	Tent	Song
1	Cro Cro	Icons	Nobody Ain't Guh Know
2	De Fosto	Kaiso Karavan	Police Money
3	Devon Seale	Revue	One Song
4	Maria Bhola	*Unattached*	I Love You
5	Chalkdust	Revue	Soca Warrior
6	Duane O'Connor	Generation Next	Sartorial Elegance
7	Sean Daniel	Generation Next	Ring
8	Skatie	Revue	Can't Have Your Cake And Eat It

Place	Artiste	Tent	Song
9	Heather Mac Intosh	*Unattached*	Check I
10	Shadow	Kaiso House	If Ah Coulda
11	Singing Sandra	Kaiso House	Sudan
12	Jervae Caesar	Generation Next	Carry Me
13	Crazy [Tie]	Revue	Paradise
13	Valentino [Tie]	Kaiso House	Pioneers
15	Black Sage	*Unattached*	Send For Somebody

The Points: 1st – 428; **2nd** – 423; **3rd** – 420; **4th** – 418; **5th** – 417; **6th** – 412; **7th** – 410; **8th** – 402; **9th** – 394; **10th** – 392; **11th** – 385; **12th** – 382; **13th** – 379 [Tie]; **15th** – 367

The Calypso Monarch Competition turned a new chapter in 2007 when a decision was taken to adopt a format dating back to the early days when calypsonians were required to sing just one song. This change was implemented in response to bitter complaints about the overwhelming number of substandard performances and slow, dreary songs which were making it to the advanced stages of the competition. The chorus of disgruntled voices seemed to have gotten louder after the 2006 Calypso Fiesta at Skinner Park in San Fernando. Then TUCO president, Michael "Protector" Legerton who led the campaign for a return to the one song format, was strong in his condemnation of the troubling trend:

> "I am hopping mad. Imagine we are supposed to be entertaining a massive crowd standing in blazing sun and what we have instead is a series of funeral marches that could not even get the people to move to the music, except for two or perhaps three contestants. If I am to shoulder full responsibility for how that show turned out-and I do-it must also be my burden to ensure this kind of thing never happens again."
>
> [**Express 20 February 2006**]

This "new" one-song format allowed 48 semi-finalists to perform before the judges at the 2007 Calypso Fiesta, 18 more than in previous years. As a natural progression the number of finalists was also increased, from 12 as was the case in 2006 to 15.

A new home, however, had to be found for the calypso final and other events traditionally staged at the Queen's Park Savannah, Port of Spain. The centerpiece of Port of Spain's carnival was declared unavailable at the end of the 2006 season to facilitate the demolition of the Grand Stand and the various other supporting buildings comprising that facility. Plans were advanced by the then People's National Movement (PNM) administration for the construction of a $450 million, ultra-modern, national carnival & entertainment centre on the site. With that plan in place and the demolition process underway the carnival landscape in Port of Spain in 2007 was altered considerably. Several of the major events traditionally held at the "Savannah" leading up to the Dimanche Gras Show on Carnival Sunday Night were staged instead at the Jean Pierre Sporting Complex in Woodbrook. The National Panorama Finals on Carnival Saturday Night were, for the first time in the history of that competition, staged at Skinner Park in San Fernando. The grand "Savannah" stage upon which hundreds of thousands of frenzied, costumed revelers pranced over the years was gone. A new/ interim central area for judging the parade of the bands was established at the south-eastern end of the "Savannah" sans any semblance of a stage. The road was the stage at that venue.

The demolition was completed later in 2007, but it was an almost total reversal in 2008. The Queen's Park Savannah was once again the main venue for the staging of pre-carnival events, including the Dimanche Gras on Carnival Sunday night, and the parade of the bands on Carnival Monday and Tuesday. A temporary structure closely resembling the demolished Grand Stand was erected. The area directly opposite, where the North Stand is built each carnival season was left open and renamed the Northern Greens, and, of course, the big savannah stage was back. To date construction is yet to begin on the proposed ultra-modern, national carnival & entertainment centre.

Sugar Aloes was noticeably absent during the 2007 season. He made a brief appearance at the Revue Tent to inform the audience that his doctors had advised him to take a two-year hiatus from performing, having undergone invasive surgery just a few months earlier. By this time he was already the official manager of the tent. A few short months later he was defiantly back on stage competing in the finals of the National Political Calypso Monarch Competition. He placed 4th singing his 2004 hit "Never Again."

Cro Cro's triumph in the 2007 calypso final was challenged by the likes of Sugar Aloes and Skatie, who accused the newly crowned monarch of contravening the rules of the competition by singing a song which he had performed 20 years ago. Those accusations were dismissed by the TUCO leadership. One week after the competition Cro Cro performed to a very receptive audience at Pan Trinbago's Champs In Concert show. The new calypso monarch, $500,000 richer, thumbed his nose at his accusers and called on them to apologize as he sang a verse of his 1995 calypso "The Apology," a new verse specially written for the occasion:

> *Doh mind ah pint size*
> *Come out and apologise*
> *Tell them is a norm*
> *Cro Cro is a master of this art form*
> *Aloes cuss*
> *Is wickedness cause his intestine to buss*
> *The cut-arse they get have them stupid*
> *All I waiting for is the Trinity Cross*

On Saturday 7th July, 2007 Cro Cro successfully defended his National Political Calypso Monarch title singing "Patrick is Boss". Joint winner, Chalkdust, sang "Screening Test." Heather Mac Intosh, Skatie and DeFosto were also finalists in that mid-year competition, placing 10th, 13th and 15th respectively. Mac Intosh sang "Check I," De Fosto did "Write It Off," and Skatie delivered "Call It Now."

Maria Bhola, Duane O'Connor, Jervae Caesar, Sean Daniel and Black Sage were first-time National Calypso Monarch finalists in 2007. Jervae Caesar is the son of deceased calypsonian Puppet Master; he placed 5th in the 2007 Young Kings Calypso Monarch Competition. He went on to claim the Young Kings title in 2009. In November 2007 Duane O'Connor was victorious in the TUCO North Zone Calypso Monarch Competition, beating out eleven competitors for the $50,000 first prize. In the first round he sang "Sartorial Elegance" in tribute to The Mighty Duke; his second-round song was "The Right Voice". Heather Mac Intosh placed fourth in this North Zone competition singing "Check I" and "One For The Fans".

First reserve Black Sage made the cut when reigning monarch, Luta, opted out of defending his title. He (Black Sage) lost to Lingo in the Extempo Monarch Final three days prior to his Dimanche Gras debut, but he has quite an impressive record as an extempo singer having won that competition on three occasions: 1995, 1999 and 2004. He was 4th in the 2007 Unattached Calypso Monarch Final.

Maria Bhola had a super 2007 season, thrashing the competition in both the NWAC Calypso Queen and the Unattached Calypso Monarch Finals with her very popular and topical "I Love You." She was also triumphant in the National Calypso Categories Final, winning the title for best political commentary calypso. Her calypso comically reports on an incident involving a clash of words between former Point Fortin MP Larry Achong and residents opposed to the construction of an aluminum smelter plant that was underway in Chatam, South Trinidad.

> The slender performer padded her gut and donned a grey wig to impersonate the MP's mannerism during a re-enactment of the meeting, as recorded by CCN TV6, which brought the house down....

Achong was investigated by police in November for allegedly mouthing an [sic] obscenities at a female protester during the meeting; however, the MP has reportedly denied that allegation saying he was telling the woman "I love you".
[Express 31 January 2007]

Bhola was also the 2007 San Juan Calypso Monarch.

Chalkdust and Skatie also competed in the political commentary category; they placed third and fourth respectively. Chalkdust sang "We And Them" and Skatie did "Can't Have Your Cake And Eat It." "If Ah Coulda" brought Shadow victory in the humourous category.

Valentino was 5th in the Veterans Calypso Monarch Final. He sang "Pioneers" and "Dis Place Nice."

Heather Mac Intosh placed 4th in the Calypso Queen Competition, and 2nd in the Unattached Calypso Monarch Finals singing "Check I."

Maria Bhola, Devon Seale, and Heather Mac Intosh are all graduates of the Junior Calypso Monarch Competition.

In 2007 Chalkdust recorded his 31st appearance in the National Calypso Monarch Final, but it was his first in over twenty-five years at a tent other than the Spektakula Promotions Calypso Tent. "Chalkie" was among the original line-up of performers when "Spektakula" first opened its doors to the public in the early 1980s. He faithfully remained with them through to the end of their run. With the decline in popularity of the traditional calypso tent in Trinidad and Tobago the management of that outfit brought an end to that aspect of their operation and have shifted their focus to promoting and staging calypso shows such as "Divas in Concert" and "Battle of the Sexes." Chalkdust, with his calypso home no longer in existence, remained unattached during the 2006 season. He has since then been attached to the Revue Tent 2007.

The 2007 calypso season was arguably Crazy's most successful in his long and storied career as a calypsonian. At age 62, apart from bringing down the house at the Revue Tent with his nightly performances, he earned himself a spot among the finalists at both the National Calypso Monarch and Groovy Soca Monarch Competitions. His phenomenally popular tune "Cold Sweat" took him to every major venue on the party circuit and every other major event that called for live entertainment, making him the envy of his contemporaries. He teamed up with legendary pan arranger Len "Boogsie" Sharpe to perform "Sharing Licks" a.k.a. "Cutarse," Phase II Pan Groove's tune of choice in the Panorama Competition. Many other steelbands also selected this "Boogsie" Sharpe/Anthony Alexis composition as their tune of choice. "Phase II" would go on to claim second place in the large band category of the national finals. With his popularity growing as the season progressed Crazy dyed his long, greying beard and continued to cash in. His list of accomplishments for the 2007 season is obviously longer than this, but the point is made that the calypso gods smiled warmly on the loveable lunatic during this particular season.

2008

Date: Sunday 3rd February
Venue: Queen's Park Savannah, Port of Spain, Trinidad & Tobago

Order of Appearance

	Artiste	Given Name
1	Sekon Alves	Sekon Alves
2	Brian London	Brian London
3	Kurt Allen	Kurt Allen
4	Stinger	Dexter Parsons
5	Singing Sandra	Sandra Des Vignes-Millington
6	Crazy	Edwin Ayoung
7	Versatile	Dorril Hector
8	Singing Francine	Francine Edwards
9	Cro Cro	Weston Rawlins
10	Sugar Aloes	Michael Osouna
11	Taylor	Walter Taylor
12	Karene Asche	Karen Asche
13	Skatie	Carlos James
14	Leslie Ann Ellis	Leslie Ann Ellis
15	Chalkdust	Dr. Hollis Liverpool

Results

Place	Artiste	Tent	Song
1	Sugar Aloes	Revue	Reflections
2	Cro Cro	Icons	Respect The Fourth King
3	Karene Asche	Generation Next	The Recipe
4	Stinger	Kaiso Karavan	Voices From The Van
5	Chalkdust	Revue	St. Joan Of Arts
6	Walter Taylor	Kaiso Karavan	Sorry
7	Leslie Ann Ellis	Magnificent Glow (Tobago)	Our Nation's Heroes
8	Brian London [Tie]	Kaiso Showcase	A Song For We

Place	Artiste	Tent	Song
8	Kurt Allen [Tie]	Icons	Last Bad John Of Kaiso
10	Singing Sandra	Kaiso House	I Stand For Trinbago
11	Skatie	Revue	Reasons
12	Versatile [Tie]	Klassic Russo	Shadow Reloaded
12	Crazy [Tie]	Revue	A Positive Message
14	Singing Francine	Kaiso Karavan	The Irony
15	Sekon Alves	Generation Next	When We Meet

Reserves: Eunice Peters and Karen Eccles

The Points: 1st – 438; 2nd – 435; 3rd – 433; 4th – 430; 5th – 426; 6th – 419; 7th – 410; 8th – 409 [Tie]; 10th – 406; 11th – 402; 12th – 393 [Tie]; 14th – 386; 15th – 380.

The Prizes: 1st – $500,000, 2nd – $250,000; 3rd – $150,000; 4th – $100,000; 5th – $75,000; 6th to 15th – $40,000.

Versatile, Sekon Alves and Taylor were first time National Calypso Monarch finalists in 2008.

Days before the National Calypso finals defending Monarch Cro Cro threatened to boycott the competition if the panel of judges was not changed. His complaints were two-fold: firstly, he argued that they had turned a deaf ear to Sugar Aloes' song "Reflections" which he alleged contains melodies from one of his (Aloes') old songs and from one of Sparrow's as well. It's important to note here that Sugar Aloes topped the field at the semifinal round of the competition. Cro Cro also claimed that the judges were trained by Chalkdust, a finalist in the competition. Chalkdust responded:

> I have never trained any of NCC or TUCO's judges in my entire life. Luta, Watchman, Short Pants and Alvin Daniell have, over the years, lectured to TUCO's judges. Since I am a competitor, I have never been given the privilege of training judges although I would love to, seeing that we have encountered over the years many errors in that field…. Cro Cro must have heard that I ran a course in calypso composition for calypsonians last year, and assumed wrongly that I trained judges. **[Sunday Guardian 10 February 2008]**

Cro Cro's bitter complaints were followed by a threat of legal action, but a meeting with the TUCO leadership and an assurance from them that the judges would be changed brought an end to his protest:

> "I have two songs that I am considering and they are both originals and all mine, with no sampling, so Aloes and company better watch out. And I hope the new judges will be aware of what the others are singing and do what is right."
> **[Newsday 3 February 2008]**

Originally slated to sing "Caribbean Heroes" he decided instead to go with "Respect The Fourth King" which he sang with some vitriol, lashing out at Sugar Aloes and his other detractors who were loud in their disagreement with the judges' decision to award him the 2007 National Calypso Monarch title. Interestingly enough he was the one at that time being accused of singing one of his old songs.

In this first verse he lays the foundation for more biting lyrics as the song progresses:

As soon as the judges announce the winner
Ah never hear bacchanal so
Aloes, Skatie and Valentino
All ah dem want half kill Cro Cro
Singing Sandra, Chalkie and Bally
They say how I sing a old song
Their heart just full of hate and envy
Tell them I'm a top notch calypsonian

So tell them, tell them, tell them doh worry with me
Ah want to send this message to Singing Sandra, Chalkie, Skatie and Bally
Tell them, tell them, tell them doh worry with me
When ah see Shadow and Valentino ah say lord only heaven knows
Tell them, tell them, tell them doh worry with me
Sparrow say Cro Cro boy wha you gwine do
They did do me the same thing too
Tell them, tell them, tell them doh worry with me
But anytime they want a kaiso showdown
Ah ready like a scorpion waiting in town

Chorus
But when they ent pick me nobody cares
I alone does go home and shed meh tears
Now the lord help me they say ah win
Have respect for the fourth king king

For special emphasis the musical accompaniment rests as the last line of the chorus is delivered; Cro Cro emphatically stating that he is a four-time winner of the competition. He is deliberately careful in pronouncing the "th" in "… Fourth King King," but the subtext is quite obvious.

Sugar Aloes performance immediately followed, heightening the unfolding drama. Although his song is aimed at then Opposition Leader Basdeo Panday he added a special verse and chorus to address Cro Cro's accusations:

Ah see on the paper and also the TV
Cro Cro accuse me for using people's melody
Some things that I don't understand about this madman
He tell heself he is the greatest calypsonian
Because he win four times he tell heself he is a champion
He say ah cannot beat him in this competition
But this year 2008 let the record show
Ah going to give him a good cut arse until he grow

Chorus
Sugar could put yuh in a coma
Look in the Mirror
He must remember Aloes bitter
Look in the mirror
He sing a song about the father
Look in the mirror
Yet still he fighting down a brother
He say all them judges were trained by Chalkie
And he not defending nothing until they change everybody
He declare war on me and Chalkie and Skatie too
So from the Revue, here's looking at you

This is just another chapter in the longstanding, bitter rivalry between Sugar Aloes and Cro Cro.

Karene Asche won the Political Calypso Category of the National Categories Calypso Competition held at "The Savannah" on the Thursday night prior to the National Calypso Monarch Finals; Sugar Aloes' was second. In the Social Commentary Category Stinger, the reigning Police Services Calypso Monarch, was first; Brian London, the South Calypso Monarch, was second, Chalkdust was third, Kurt Allen was fourth and Singing Francine was fifth. The songs were the same as those performed at the National Finals listed above.

Leslie Ann Ellis won both the Tobago Calypso Monarch Competition and the Tobago Calypso Queen titles with "Our Nation's Heroes".

2009

Date: Sunday 22nd February
Venue: Queen's Park Savannah, Port of Spain, Trinidad & Tobago

Order of Appearance

	Artiste	Given Name
1	Stinger	Dexter Parsons
2	Karene Asche	Karene Asche
3	Contender	Mark John
4	Singing Sandra	Sandra Des Vignes-Millington
5	De Fosto	Winston Scarborough
6	All Rounder	Anthony Hendrickson
7	Chalkdust	Dr. Hollis Liverpool
8	Sugar Aloes	Michael Osouna
9	Tigress	Joanne Rowley
10	Twiggy	Ann Marie Parks-Kojo
11	Gypsy	Winston Peters
12	Brian London	Brian London
13	Cro Cro	Weston Rawlins
14	Bally	Errol Ballantyne
15	Skatie	Carlos James
16	Kizzie Ruiz	Kizzie Ruiz

Results

Place	Artiste	Tent	Song
1	Chalkdust	Revue	My Hart And I
2	Tigress	Icons	You Ent See Wajang Yet
3	De Fosto	Kaiso Karavan	Could We Rise Again
4	Brian London	Icons	A Nation's Son
5	Kizzie Ruiz	Generation Next	Class Language
6	Singing Sandra	Kaiso House	Ghetto Of Your Mind
7	Gypsy	Kaiso House	Supply And Demand
8	Sugar Aloes	Revue	Obama The First

Place	Artiste	Tent	Song
9	Twiggy	Kaiso House	One For Obama
10	Karene Asche	Generation Next	Babylon
11	Stinger	Kaiso Karavan	Our Environmental Engineers
12	Skatie	Revue	On Solid Ground
13	Cro Cro	Icons	Ah Feeling Shame
14	All Rounder	Klassic Ruso	Help Your Children First
15	Contender	Klassic Ruso	Yuh Cyar Buy One
16	Bally	Revue	Amigo

Reserves: Kurt Allen and Candice Robinson

The Prizes: 1st – $500,000, **2nd** – $250,000; **3rd** – $150,000; **4th** – $100,000; **5th** – $75,000; **6th** to **16th** – $40,000.

With his performance of "My Hart And I" Chalkdust scored his eighth National Calypso King/Monarch victory, placing him alongside King of the Calypso World, The Mighty Sparrow, who is the only other calypsonian to have achieved such a feat.

> Now that I have equalled Sparrow's record I am thinking of bowing out of the competition, out of respect for Sparrow. I have no desire to break his record because of what he means to calypso and all he has achieved through the years. My circle of friends are, however, telling me not to go. It's not that they want me to break the record, but because they believe the competition will lose some of its essence if I go. **[Express 24 February 2009]**

As noble as the gesture was, Chalkdust eventually decided against retirement from the competition. He recorded his first win in 1976 with "Why Smut" and "Ah Put On Meh Guns" while Sparrow's last winning performance was in 1992 when he sang "Survival" and "Both Of Them". Chalkdust stands today as the only person with any realistic chance of breaking the record. His closest rival is The Black Stalin whose last victory, his fifth, was in 1995 when he sang "In Time" and "Sundar". In September of 2014 Stalin suffered a stroke and has not performed since. One year earlier, in September of 2013, Sparrow was similarly afflicted. He has since recovered and continues to perform despite his considerably weakened physical condition which puts paid to any thought of him returning to the national calypso competition. Sparrow last appeared in the finals in 1995; he placed third singing "Democracy In Haiti" and "This Is Madness". Cro Cro was second with "The Apology" and "Jump And Wave". Should Chalkie score just one more victory and retire from the competition his record of nine victories will stand for a considerably long period of time.

Sparrow	Chalkdust
1956 - Jean and Dinah	1976 - Why Smut / Ah Put On Meh Guns
1960 - Ten To One Is Murder / Mae Mae	1977 - My Kind Of Protest / Shango Vision
1962 - Federation / Sparrow Come Back Home	1981 - Things That Worry Me / Ah Cyar Make
1963 - Dan Is The Man / Kennedy	1989 - Chauffeur Wanted / Carnival Is The Answer
1972 - Drunk And Disorderly / Rope	1993 - Kaiso In The Hospital / Misconception
1973 - School Days / Same Time Same Place	2004 - Trinidad In The Cemetery / Fish Mongrel
1974 - We Pass That Stage / Miss Mary	2005 - I In Town Too Long / Ah Doh Rhyme
1992 - Survival / Both Of Them	2009 - My Hart And I

Joint holders of the record for Calypso King/Monarch victories

The scoring system used to determine the placing was put to the test in 2009, bringing with it some controversy. Under this system the highest and lowest scores for each singer are removed. The aggregate of the remaining scores (the net score) is recorded as the final score. In the event of a tie the dropped scores are added back in for a total score which hopefully will separate the tied contestants.

At the 2009 competition after the highest and lowest scores were removed for each singer the net scores were as follows:

1st – 434; **2nd** – 426; **3rd** – 425; **4th** – 424; **5th** – 414; **6th** – 412; **7th** – 409; **7th** – 409; **7th** – 409; **10th** – 401; **11th** – 400; **12th** – 397; **13th** – 396; **13th** – 396; **15th** – 302; **16th** – 386.

Twiggy, Sugar Aloes and Gypsy were tied at 409 points and Cro Cro and All Rounder were at 396 points each. The tie-breaking procedure was implemented giving Gypsy seventh place with a total score of 584 points, Sugar Aloes 8th with 578 points and Twiggy 9th with 570 points. Breaking the other tie, Cro Cro secured 13th place with a total score of 560 points and All Rounder claimed the 14th spot with 550 total points. These total scores affected the placing of just the tied contestants; there was no bearing on the rest of the results. As fate would have it, though, a breakdown in communication between those presiding over the tie-breaking procedure and the person or persons responsible for relaying the official results to the house announcer resulted in an inaccurate announcement going out to the public:

> AN ERROR in communication on Dimanche Gras night resulted in five competitors being announced as having tied, when in fact their scores went through a tie-breaking procedure, Trinbago Unified Calypsonian Organization (TUCO) Secretary General Lutalo "Brother Resistance" Masimba said yesterday. But in immediate reaction former defending Calypso Monarch Michael "Sugar Aloes" Osouna raised allegations of tampering with the official results.
> **[Newsday 26 February 2009]**

The mix up also led to various incorrect versions of the results being published in the press and on internet websites.

The calypso world mourned the passing of The Mighty Duke on January 14th 2009, he was 76. Chalkdust, his very good friend of many years, was at his bedside when he passed on; so too were Duke's wife, Rebecca John-Pope and his son Wendell. Chalkie delivered the eulogy at the funeral service.

Duke's record of four consecutive wins (1968-1971) stands unbroken to this day; it was challenged only by The Mighty Sparrow's streak of wins from 1972 to 1974. Chalkdust dedicated his 2009 victory song to his good friend.

Twiggy and Contender were first time National Calypso Monarch finalists in 2009.

In 2009 Twiggy scored her second victory in the National Women's Action Committee's Calypso Queen Competition. She was NWAC's first calypso queen in 1985 when responsibility for staging the competition was passed on to that organization. She won with "Life" and "The Outside Woman". In 2009 her winning song was "One For Obama"; Karene Asche placed second singing "In The Abundance Of Water", and Kizzie Ruiz took third place with "Class Language."

Contender secured second place in the Veterans Calypso Monarch Competition; he sang "Yuh Cyar Buy One" and "Young And Restless". He was also a finalist in the National Extempo Competition.

Tigress won the prize for best political song in TUCO's Calypso Categories Competition; she sang "You Ent See Wajang Yet". All Rounder placed third in the political category and fourth in the social commentary category. Brian London won the social commentary category with "A Nation's Song". Stinger, the reigning Police Calypso Monarch, took second place and Twiggy was third.

Brian London successfully defended his title in the South Calypso Monarch Competition. He also became South's first Extempo champ.

After several years away from the calypso scene, Gypsy returned to a warm welcome from most audiences. In the National Extempo Competition he placed second to visually impaired singer, Lingo, who scored a hat trick of wins with that victory. Gypsy himself is a former Extempo champ, having won this competition on several occasions in the past. He turned the tables on Lingo in 2010, beating him as they met again in the final. They would match wits again as finalists six years later as Gypsy returned to competition following the hiatus he took during his tenure as a minister of government. Lingo was once again beaten into second place.

2010

Date: Sunday 14th February
Venue: Queen's Park Savannah, Port of Spain, Trinidad & Tobago

Order of Appearance

	Artiste	Given Name
1	Mistah Shak	Selvon Noel
2	Skatie	Carlos James
3	Chalkdust	Dr. Hollis Liverpool
4	Brian London	Brian London
5	Singing Sandra	Sandra Des Vignes-Millington
6	De Fosto	Winston Scarborough
7	Protector	Michael Legerton
8	Sean Daniel	Sean Daniel
9	Devon Seale	Devon Seale
10	Mr. Chucky	Roderick Gordon
11	All Rounder	Anthony Hendrickson
12	Twiggy	Ann Marie Parks-Kojo
13	Kizzie Ruiz	Kizzie Ruiz
14	Nicole Greaves	Nicole Greaves
15	Kurt Allen	Kurt Allen

Results

Place	Artiste	Tent	Song
1	Kurt Allen	Icons	Too Bright
2	Brian London	Kaiso House	A Calypsonian
3	De Fosto	Kaiso Karavan	In A Palace State Of Mind
4	Kizzie Ruiz	*Unattached*	Aide Haiti
5	Mr. Chucky	Kaiso House	A People's National Movement
6	Chalkdust	Revue	When Mas Was Mas
7	Mistah Shak	Kaiso House	Rogue
8	Nicole Greaves	Revue	Where The Lions Are

Place	Artiste	Tent	Song
9	Sean Daniel	Revue	God Is Love
10	Singing Sandra	Kaiso House	No Child Shall Be Left Behind
11	Twiggy	Kaiso House	Give Thanks
12	Devon Seale	Revue	A Wind Of Change
13	Skatie	Revue	Cry For Life
14	Protector	Kaiso Showcase	My Vision
15	All Rounder	Klassic Ruso	Female Lifeguard

The Prizes: 1st – $500,000, **2nd** – $250,000; **3rd** – $150,000; **4th** – $100,000; **5th** – $75,000; **6th** to **15th** – $40,000.

Nicole Greaves and Mistah Shak were first time National Calypso Monarch finalists in 2010.

Kurt Allen was a reserve in 2009; in 2010 he added National Calypso Monarch to his other major titles. He was crowned Young King in 1993 and International Soca Monarch in 1999.

Brian London retained his National Carnival Commission Regional Calypso Monarch title in Diego Martin. A few days later he was crowned the South Calypso Monarch at Skinner Park in San Fernando; that was his sixth win in that competition (2004, 2005, 2006, 2008, 2009, 2010). He also successfully defended his South Extempo Monarch title on the same night.

From a field of eighteen female calypsonians Kizzie Ruiz emerged triumphant in the National Women's Action Committee (NWAC) Calypso Queen Competition; she performed "Aide Haiti". Nicole Greaves placed second singing "Where The Lions Are".

Kizzie was also in winners' row at the Kaisorama Show at the Queen's Park Savannah three nights prior to her National Calypso Monarch performance on Carnival Sunday Night. She won the title for Best Social Commentary song in the Calypso Categories segment of the show; Brian London took second place. De Fosto was the winner in the Political class, Kurt Allen was second and Chalkdust was third. All Rounder was third in the Humourous category which was won by Short Pants who sang "The Infidel". Crazy placed second with "For Carnival." With the exception of "Eye Problems" which was sung by Chalkdust, all other songs performed were the same as those listed above for each respective artiste.

2011

Date: Sunday 6th March
Venue: Queen's Park Savannah, Port of Spain, Trinidad & Tobago

Order of Appearance

	Artiste	Given Name
1	Cro Cro	Weston Rawlins
2	Kizzie Ruiz	Kizzie Ruiz
3	Stinger	Dexter Parsons
4	Kurt Allen	Kurt Allen
5	Karene Acshe	Karene Asche
6	Chalkdust	Dr. Hollis Liverpool
7	Devon Seale	Devon Seale
8	Tigress	Joanne Rowley
9	Sugar Aloes	Michael Osouna
10	Tameka Darius	Tameka Darius
11	Benjai	Rodney le Blanc
12	Brian London	Brian London

Results

Place	Artiste	Tent	Song 1	Song 2
1	Karene Asche	Kaiso House	Careful What You Ask For	Uncle Jack
2	Sugar Aloes	Revue	De Cause	Not One Word
3	Chalkdust	Revue	Wounded Pride	Power Of The Pen
4	Devon Seale	Revue	Retro Rama	Ah Need Meh Carnival
5	Stinger	Kaiso Karavan	Mystic Revelations	2,000,000 Reasons
6	Kurt Allen	Icons	Do So	Tribute To Atilla The Hun
7	Brian London	Kaiso House	We Fed Up	Fly High
8	Tameka Darius	Revue	Tomorrow	Ungrateful
9	Kizzie Ruiz	*Unattached*	The Anti-Corruption Cure	De Engine Stall

Place	Artiste	Tent	Song 1	Song 2
10	Tigress	Revue	A Mature Woman	Woman To Woman
11	Cro Cro	Icons	Compare And Contrast	Kam-Lie
12	Benjai	*Unattached*	Wine To The Side	Trini

Tameka Darius and Benjai were newcomers to the calypso finals in 2011.

After years of debate there was a return to the two-song format at the calypso monarch finals. In 2007 a decision was taken to limit the performances to just one song, giving in to loud complaints pouring in year after year about the poor quality of songs being performed at the advanced stages of the competition. The reintroduced two-song format applies only to the final stage of the competition however.

A new system of judging was also introduced in 2011. Under the old system there was one panel of seven judges who assessed each performance based on the following criteria: Lyrics (30 points); Melody (30 points); Rendition (20 points); Presentation (10 points); and Originality (10 points) for a possible total of 100 points from each judge. The high and low scores for each performance dropped to offset any bias that may exist.

Under the new system assessment is based on three broad-based criteria, employing a panel of five judges for each criterion. (Total of fifteen judges)

> **Lyrics (40 points):** Topic; Depth of Idea; Development of Theme; Structure; Introduction To Topic; Coherence; Skilful Utilization of Figures of Speech; Clarity of Diction.
>
> **Music (40 points):** Melody Line; Originality and Compatibility; Orchestration; Horn Arrangements; Use of Rhythm; Articulation; Perfect Pitch; Voice Quality; Use of Background Vocals; Harmony and Unison.
>
> **Presentation (20 points):** Stage Presence; Use of Creative Mechanisms To Enhance Performance.

The high and low scores in each criterion are dropped to offset any bias that may exist; the average of the three remaining scores are totaled to arrive at each contestant's score out of a 100 point total. The contestant with the highest score is declared the winner.

The 2011 Points: 1st – 489, **2nd** – 481, **3rd** – 468, **4th** – 467, **5th** – 462, **6th** – 461, **7th** – 455, **8th** – 444, **9th** – 443, **10th** – 436, **11th** – 417, **12th** – 405.

In 2011 there was a significant spike in the prize money awarded to the Calypso Monarch; to date it is the biggest purse in the history of the competition. Living up to a campaign promise, the then newly elected People's Partnership Government of Trinidad and Tobago sponsored the first prize of $2,000,000 TTD for four of the country's major carnival competitions; (Chutney Soca Monarch, Panorama, Power Soca Monarch and the National Calypso Monarch).

The Prizes: 1st – $2,000,000, **2nd** – 500,000, **3rd** – $250,000, **4th** – $150,000, **5th** – $100,000, **6th to 12th** – $60,000.

Karene Asche's historic victory came just days after she won the title for Best Political Song in the Calypso Categories segment of TUCO's Kaisorama Competition. This was held at the Queen's Park Savannah, on Thursday March 3rd. Karene sang "Uncle Jack"; Chalkdust placed third with "Manningitis". Devon Seale won the social commentary category with "Ah Need Meh Carnival".

Karene Asche receiving her first prize cheque from then Prime Minister Kamla Persad-Bissessar. Also in the photo from left to right are: Wade Madre, King of Carnival 2011, Winston Peters aka the Mighty Gypsy, Minister of The Arts and Multiculturalism, and Lutalo Masimba, President of TUCO. Partially hidden at the back are Vasant Bharath then Minister of Food Production, Land and Marine Affairs and Attorney General Anand Ramlogan. *Photo provided by TriniSoca.com*

Brian London etched his name in the annals of calypso lore as the "winningest" South Calypso Monarch. Singing "We Fed Up" at Skinner Park in San Fernando on Wednesday 2nd March 2011 he captured his 7th South Calypso Monarch title, completing the beaver-trick (2008, 2009, 2010 and 2011) which follows his earlier hat trick of wins (2004, 2005 and 2006). He opted out of the competition in 2007.

Benjai's placing in the calypso finals doesn't reflect it, but he enjoyed what arguably was his most successful carnival season to date. As a soca artiste with two of the season's biggest hits there was hardly a carnival event of note that didn't include him. And amid the revelry he entered and won the Young Kings Calypso Competition (TT$100,000 prize), placed second in the Groovy Soca Monarch Competition (TT$225,000), and banked an additional TT$60,000 for his placing in the National Calypso Monarch Finals on Carnival Sunday Night.

Notwithstanding his placing, Benjai's selection to the calypso monarch finals must be viewed as a major accomplishment. Soca artistes seldom get the opportunity to compete against the traditional calypsonians, especially so with respect to this particular competition. One would have to look back thirteen years prior to Benjai's 2011 performance to find Wayne Rodriguez in the 1998 final, singing "Set

My Music Free" and that year's road march song, "Footsteps". He tied for 9th place with Luta. Rodriguez died of an apparent suicide in September 2001.

Benjai's hugely popular "Trini" joins the growing list of patriotic songs affectionately referred to as unofficial national anthems of Trinidad and Tobago, but its popularity was not without controversy. The melody of this song was built around a heavy sample of Ed Watson's 1979 hit "You Gotta Give Away" sung by Singing Diane. Soon after its release a chorus of dissenting voices was loud in their condemnation of what in their view was a blatant case of copyright infringement. Ed Watson himself confirmed that the music was used without his permission; he instructed the Copyright Organization of Trinidad and Tobago (COTT) to step in on his behalf and after some to-ing and fro-ing an eventual settlement was agreed upon.

"Trini" was produced by the New York-based Art and Life Studios.

2012

Date: Sunday 19th February
Venue: Queen's Park Savannah, Port of Spain, Trinidad & Tobago

Order of Appearance

	Artiste	Given Name
1	Sugar Aloes	Michael Osouna
2	Singing Sandra	Sandra Des Vignes Millington
3	Kurt Allen	Kurt Allen
4	Karene Asche	Karene Asche
5	Cro Cro	Weston Rawlins
6	Chalkdust	Dr. Hollis Liverpool
7	Devon Seale	Devon Seale
8	Leslie Ann Ellis	Leslie Ann Ellis
9	Heather Mac Intosh	Heather Mac Intosh
10	Stinger	Dexter Parsons
11	Brian London	Brian London
12	Duane O'Connor	Duane O'Connor

Results

Place	Artiste	Tent	Song 1	Song 2
1	Duane O'Connor	Kaiso House	The Hunt Is On	Long Live Calypso
2	Kurt Allen	Icons	Long Live Calypso	It Is A Ledged
3	Karene Asche	Kaiso House	Against All Odds	You Will Win D Battle But
4	Devon Seale	Revue	One Is One	Snapshot
5	Heather Mac Intosh	Icons	The Adjective	One Gone
6	Chalkdust	Revue	Shame Mr Shak	How's Dat
7	Sugar Aloes	Revue	Doh Force Meh Hand	Chinese Kidnapping
8	Stinger	Kaiso Karavan	My Reason For Being Here	Advice In Song
9	Brian London	Kaiso House	Not Brian	Doh Complain – Come Plain
10	Singing Sandra	Kaiso House	On Turing 50	Why I Sing

Place	Artiste	Tent	Song 1	Song 2
11	Leslie Ann Ellis	Magnificent Glow (Tobago)	Street Justice	Mothers And Others
12	Cro Cro	Icons	Say Something	Release them

The Prizes: **1st** – $1,000,000, **2nd** – 500,000, **3rd** – $275,000, **4th** – $175,000, **5th** – $100,000, **6th** to **12th** – $60,000.

The Points: **1st** – 522, **2nd** – 502, **3rd** – 500, **4th** – 492, **5th** – 488, **6th** – 477, **7th** – 474, **8th** – 473, **9th** – 472, **10th** – 471, **11th** – 469, **12th** – 468.

Throughout the history of the national calypso contest calypsonians have had to raise their voices in protest, mainly over the prize money offered to them. The Sparrow-led boycott of 1957 seems to have set a precedent in such matters. In 2012, as was the case in 1957, the burning issue was parity with other national competitions:

> Seven of the 12 calypsonians who are supposed to perform tomorrow night at the National Calypso Monarch Finals Dimanche Gras yesterday warned that if the prize monies are not raised, there may not be a calypso competition at "the big yard", Queens Park Savannah…. Sandra Des Vignes Millington aka "Singing Sandra", Weston Rawlins aka "Cro Cro" and Brian London, Devon Seales [sic], defending monarch Karene Asche (who last year won $2 million- a one-time prize figure by the Government for that year alone), Duane O'Connor and Dexter Parsons aka Stinger are the calypsonians who declared their intentions. [**Newsday 18 February 2012**]

> The calypsonians yesterday during the draw for positions at the Kaiso House calypso tent, Queen's Park Savannah declared unanimously that to offer a first prize of only $500,000 when other competitions such as the Chutney Soca Monarch and the International Power Soca Monarch were giving first prizes of $1 million and $2 million respectively was a gross insult to the art form and the calypsonians. [**Express 18 February 2012**]

The threatened boycott was called off after a last minute deal was struck and it was announced that the prize money was increased:

> With just hours to go before the start of the National Calypso Monarch competition and with calypsonians threatening to boycott the show, an agreement to increase the first prize from $500,000 to $1 million was hammered out.

> "This is good for calypso. Calypso is the father of all the different genres of music, so they must ensure that calypso gets a good prize. All these other genres of music: chutney, soca, they all came out of calypso, so it's only fair that calypsonians get a good prize," said finalist in the National Calypso Monarch competition, Dr Hollis "Chalkdust" Liverpool, in response to the news of the increased prize. [**Express 20 February 2012**]

The year 2012 signaled the coming-of-age for Duane O'Connor who, after years of knocking on the door, finally found the right combination. At the end of the season he added to an already impressive résumé the following titles: Eastern Credit Union Calypso Monarch, TUCO North Zone Calypso Monarch, NACC Young Kings Calypso Monarch, and the most treasured, Trinidad and Tobago National Calypso Monarch. He holds the distinction of being the first and only member of the Trinidad and Tobago Police Service to date to have won the National Calypso Competition.

O'Connor also walked away with the top prize in the Social Commentary Category of the 2012 edition of Kaisorama singing "The Hunt Is On". Kurt Allen was second with "When Will It End" and Chalkdust placed third with "How's Dat". In the Political Commentary Category Kurt Allen took the top prize singing "Long Live Calypso"; Heather Mac Intosh was second with "The Adjective" and Bunny B took third place with "Political Lightning". In the Extempo Category Brian London was beaten into second place by Lady Africa; Lingo was third.

Sugar Aloes was a finalist at the 2012 National Humor Calypso Monarch Competition; he placed third singing "Chinese Kidnapping" and "Gas". The Incredible Myron B claimed the title with "Baby Roll Over" and "Ah Fraid For Meh Life". Second was veteran calypsonian Composer who sang "Legacy" and "Waist Talent".

By sheer coincidence it seems both Duane O'Connor and Kurt Allen sang "Long Live Calypso" at the 2012 National Calypso Monarch Final. O'Connor won the title and Allen placed second. Three years later at the 2015 final it was Queen Victoria's turn, her second song bearing an identical title. It must be pointed out, though, that apart from the general sentiments expressed about the calypso genre, each song is as different from the other as can be when taking lyrics, melody and tempo into account. It is interesting to note as well that throughout the history of the competition several other similar instances can be found. At the 1958 final both The Mighty Skipper and Pretender sang "Federation"; most of us may only be familiar with Sparrow's "Federation" of the 1962 final which he won. Then there is "Maria" which was one of Blakie's songs at that 1962 final where he placed seventh. Sparrow's "Maria" dates back to 1960. In both songs the bards are lovesick over a girl by the name of Maria. In 1982 Designer's second song in the final was "Not A Damn Seat For Them". Pretender, although not making it to the final, also sang "Not A Damn Seat For Dem" that year, but it is Kitchener's "Not A Damn Seat For Dem" most of us may be able to recall. Kitchener, by this time had retired from competition. At the 1971 final Superior's second song was "Respect Calypsonians"; Gypsy's first song as a finalist in 1988 was "Respect The Calypsonian". Ella Andall at the 1996 final did "Rhythm Of A People" as her second song; the following year would find Gypsy winning the title; his first song was "Rhythm Of A People". That was the year of the "Little Black Boy". Finally, Crazy in 2007 and Helon Francis in 2016 did "Paradise".

Looking at the phenomenon of final night similarities from a different perspective brings the 2016 final into focus with Heather Mac Intosh's performance of "By Other Men's Faults" and Cro Cro's "Advice To D Boss". In both songs the calypsonian is advising the recently elected Prime Minister Rowley to avoid the missteps of former Prime Minister Kamla Persad-Bissessar. In both instances as part of the presentation of the song an actor playing the role of PM Rowley with pen and notepad in hand took notes as the singer listed the transgressions of the former PM and her ministers.

2013

Date: Thursday 7th February
Venue: Queen's Park Savannah, Port of Spain, Trinidad & Tobago

Order of Appearance

	Artiste	Given Name
1	Kurt Allen	Kurt Allen
2	Queen Victoria	Victoria Cooper
3	Karene Asche	Karene Asche
4	Duane O'Connor	Duane O'Connor
5	Pink Panther	Eric Taylor
6	Chalkdust	Dr. Hollis Liverpool
7	Kizzie Ruiz	Kizzie Ruiz
8	Eunice Peters	Eunice Peters
9	Heather Mac Intosh	Heather Mac Intosh
10	Marvelous Marva	Marva Joseph
11	Mr. Chucky	Roderick Gordon
12	Alana Sinnette-Khan	Alana Sinnette-Khan

Results

Place	Artiste	Tent	Song 1	Song 2
1	Pink Panther	Revue	Travel Woes	Crying In The Chapel
2	Kurt Allen	Kaiso Karavan	Political Sin-Phony	Black Stalin Say
3	Heather Mac Intosh	Icons	The Old Man's Lament	Invisible
4	Mr. Chucky	Kaiso House	Bear With Me	The New Addiction
5	Karene Asche	Kaiso House	Meh Pardner Ship	Eat Ah Food
6	Eunice Peters	Kaiso Karavan	None Of The Above	Keshorn D Javelin Champion
7	Duane O'Connor	Kaiso House	Building A Wall	Seeking Sparrow's Advice
8	Alana Sinnette-Khan	Revue	No Moral Authority	Pathological
9	Chalkdust	Revue	Prodigal Son	Virginia's Alzheimer
10	Kizzie Ruiz	*Unattached*	In The Age Of Blog	T And T Forever

Place	Artiste	Tent	Song 1	Song 2
11	Marvelous Marva	Kaiso House	Come Back To What	Woman's Contribution To Trinidad And Tobago
12	Queen Victoria	Kaiso Showkase	D Betrayal	Club 34

The Prizes: 1st – $1,000,000, **2nd** – 500,000, **3rd** – $275,000, **4th** – $175,000, **5th** – $100,000, **6th** to **12th** – $60,000.

Alana Sinnette-Khan and Queen Victoria were first-time National Calypso Monarch finalists in 2013.

For the second time in its history the national calypso final was held on the Thursday before carnival. The first was on Thursday 19th February 1998 when Mystic Prowler won the title singing "Look Below The Surface" and "Vision Of T&T In The Year 2010". The following year saw a return to the traditional Carnival Sunday Night, Dimanche Gras setting. This was kept in place all the way through to the 2012 finals. The decision to revisit the Thursday night scenario in 2013 was based on an idea pitched by TUCO according to Allison Demas, then Chairman of the National Carnival Commission:

> Changes to the Dimanche Gras were made at an annual general meeting of the Trinbago Unified Calypsonians Organisation (TUCO) in September 2011 by the general membership, with a motion raised by the executive that there should be a separate show for the Calypso Monarch .... Demas said the idea behind the separation of the shows was to take a step towards achieving some measure of financial viability.
> [Sunday Express 17 February 2013]

Although Demas was quoted as saying that the Dimanche Gras "will remain a non-competitive event", by the following year the crowning of the National Calypso Monarch was once again the main focus of the Carnival Sunday Night event. The celebration of the 100th anniversary of the first vocal recording of Calypso formed the theme of the 2014 Dimanche Gras show (see page 81).

Pink Panther walked away with calypso's most prestigious title on his fourth trip to the national finals. Both his songs were written by Chalkdust. Pink Panther was also a big winner in 1992 when he won the National Action Cultural Committee's Young Kings Calypso Competition. He sang "Why Ah Change" and "Back To Her Majesty". Kurt Allen was also a Young Kings finalist in 1992; he placed 4th with "Subconsciously" and "Take The Dragon Down".

At the 2013 National Calypso Monarch Finals another breakthrough moment for female calypsonians was recorded. It was the first time in the history of the competition that the male finalists were outnumbered by their female counterparts. After a strong showing at Calypso Fiesta in Skinner Park (the semifinal round of the competition) where nineteen of the forty semifinalists were female; seven of them were selected among the twelve finalists. This in itself was another milestone for the ladies as there have never been more than five female combatants in the final round. Calypso Rose was the first female finalist in 1968, she placed 5th in a field of seven, beating the Mighty Cypher and Lord Baker into 6th and 7th respectively. Rose sang "Fire In She Wire" and "Pudding Man". In the history of this competition twenty-five females to date have made it to the final round at least once. Among them Singing Sandra leads with fourteen appearances (see Appendix C-ii). One hundred and sixteen male calypsonians to date have been to the final round (see Appendix A-ii).

The ladies have taken top honours on five occasions:

Calypso Rose 1978
(Her Majesty / I Thank Thee)
Singing Sandra 1999
(Song For Healing / Voices From The Ghetto)
Denyse Plummer 2001
(Heroes / Nah Leaving)
Singing Sandra 2003
(For Whom The Bell Tolls / Ancient Rhythms)
Karene Asche 2011
(Careful What You Ask For / Uncle Jack)

The Ladies of the Trinidad and Tobago National Calypso Monarch Finals

Calypso Rose

Singing Francine

Singing Dianne

Buzzing Bee

Princess Natasha

Denyse Plummer

Eastlyn Orr

Abbi Blackman

Singing Sonia

The Ladies of the Trinidad and Tobago National Calypso Monarch Finals

Singing Sandra

Ella Andall

Tigress

Heather Mac Intosh

Kizzie Ruiz

Leslie Ann Ellis

Karene Asche

Maria Bhola

Twiggy

The Ladies of the Trinidad and Tobago National Calypso Monarch Finals

Nicole Greaves

Tameka Darius

Queen Victoria

Eunice Peters

Marvelous Marva

Alana Sinnette Khan

Lady Adanna

Photo Credit

Buzzing Bee
Reprinted with permission of Emile Borde

Eastlyn Orr
Reprinted with permission from National Women Action Committee

Ella Andall
Singing Dianne
Singing Sonia
Maria Bhola

Tameka Darius
Alana Sinnette Khan
Reprinted with permission of trinisoca.com

Calypso Rose
Singing Francine
Princess Natasha
Denyse Plummer
Abbi Blackman
Singing Sandra
Tigress
Heather Mac Intosh

Kizzie Ruiz
Leslie Ann Ellis
Karene Asche
Twiggy
Nicole Greaves
Queen Victoria
Eunice Peters
Marvelous Marva
Lady Adanna
Reprinted with permission of Gary Cardinez

Not making it to the final round of the national finals in 2013 was perennial favourite, Sugar Aloes, whose unstinting support for the People's National Movement (PNM) is well documented in his calypsoes through the years. In 2012 he was shooting from the hip (pun intended) with a stinging attack on the Kamla Persad-Bissessar led People's Partnership Government. Persad-Bissessar, in 2010, led a coalition of parties to unseat the PNM from political power. At the semi-final round of the competition in San Fernando Sugar Aloes did not disappoint an expectant crowd with his performance on the Skinner Park stage playing the role of a western gunslinger as he delivered his calypso:

> Even before his position was called, fans kept calling for Aloes to grace the stage. Beginning his song Doh Force Meh Hand with a spaghetti western motif, he lambasted Housing Minister Roodal Moonilal who was also at the show, Persad-Bissessar and Education Minister Tim Gopeesingh.
> **[Trinidad Guardian 13 February 2012]**

At the finals, performing in first position, he stepped it up a notch to complete the western imagery, riding a horse on stage before delivering his song. A mere three months later, however, Aloes was singing a different song:

> The bombshell of last night's People's Partnership second anniversary rally turned out to be two-time Calypso Monarch Michael "Sugar Aloes" Osuna's [sic] surprise serenade of Prime Minister Kamla Persad-Bissessar. Osuna [sic] has been an ardent supporter of the Opposition People's National Movement and vocal critic of the People's Partnership, particularly of the majority party of the coalition, the United National Congress. However, last evening he had the mammoth crowd gathered at Mid Centre Mall, Chaguanas swaying in delight as he sang Taurrus Riley's reggae hit "She's Royal" in tribute to Persad-Bissessar, whom he brought out on stage dancing.

> "She's royal, so royal," sang Osuna [sic], with the crowd singing along. His performance set the mood for Persad-Bissessar's feature address moments after.
> **[Newsday 25 May 2012]**

This about-face support for Prime Minister Persad-Bissessar brought him the wrath of many in 2013, especially so during his performance at the Calypso Fiesta where many who fail the acid test of the Skinner Park audience are treated to boos and jeers complete with rolls of toilet paper held high and signs bearing words of derision. For Aloes the reception seemed to be especially vitriolic:

> Osuna [sic], a longtime supporter of the People's National Movement (PNM) which is currently in Opposition, was targeted … by the spectators who not only threw toilet paper at him but also a roti in a clear show their displeasure at him performing recently at UNC functions where he serenaded UNC leader and Prime Minister Kamla Persad-Bissessar with the Taurrus Riley hit, 'She's So Royal'.
> **[Newsday 5 February 2013]**

Among those showing their displeasure were some of Sugar Aloes' most ardent fans who he had even celebrated in song in earlier times. The Original De Fosto Himself who had also shown support for the People's Partnership Government, came in for similar treatment from the Skinner Park crowd.

> TUCO president Lutalo Masimba expressed "strong censure" of the extremely unpleasant actions and behaviour of some members of the audience. "Such actions went beyond the realm of good taste and propriety and cannot be condoned against our artistes in any way whatsoever," Masimba said.
> **[Newsday 5 February 2013]**

Sugar Aloes makes a dramatic entrance for his performance of "Doh Force Meh Hand" at the 2012 Calypso Finals at the Queen's Park Savannah
Photo provided by TriniSoca.com

On August 25th 2012 Mr. Chucky was crowned Trinidad and Tobago's 50th Anniversary of Independence Calypso Monarch. Female calypsonians were in the majority.

The results are as follows:

1st	($ 500,000)	Mr. Chucky	"Bear With Me"
2nd	($ 250,000)	Michelle Henry	"Our National Watchwords"
3rd	($ 150,000)	Karen Eccles	"Give, I Will Reciprocate"
4th	($ 50,000)	Heather Mac Intosh	"The Reason"
5th	($ 50,000)	Kizzie Ruiz	"T&T Forever"
6th	($ 50,000)	Karene Asche	"Cascadoo"
7th	($ 50,000)	Sugar Aloes	"Team T And T"
8th	($ 50,000)	Singing Sandra	"Red, White and Black"
9th	($ 50,000)	Duane O'Connor	"Unity In Independence"
10th	($ 50,000)	King Luta	"Fifty Fifty"

The boos and jeers were just as loud for Sugar Aloes as he had experienced earlier in the year.

2014

Date: Sunday 2nd March
Venue: Queen's Park Savannah, Port of Spain, Trinidad & Tobago

Order of Appearance

	Artiste	Given Name
1	Pink Panther	Eric Taylor
2	Skatie	Carlos James
3	The Incredible Myron B	Myron Bruce
4	Mistah Shak	Selvon Noel
5	Brian London	Brian London
6	Queen Victoria	Victoria Cooper
7	Alana Sinnette-Khan	Alana Sinnette-Khan
8	Chucky	Roderick Gordon
9	Cro Cro	Weston Rawlins
10	Bodyguard	Roger Mohammed
11	Chalkdust	Dr. Hollis Liverpool
12	Kurt Allen	Kurt Allen

Results

Place	Artiste	Tent	Song 1	Song 2
1	Chucky	Kaiso House	Wah Yuh Think	Wedding Of De Century
2	Kurt Allen	Kaiso Karavan	Sweet Sizzling Summer	The Lost Psalm Of King David
3	Mistah Shak	Kaiso House	Bois	Crime Round De Clock
4	Chalkdust	Revue	Ah Miss De Bards	De Guest List
5	Brian London	Revue	The Heart Of A Warrior	Call Dem Out
6	Queen Victoria	Kaiso Showkase	Political Love Affair	Congo Warrior
7	Alana Sinnette-Khan	Revue	Sealots	And Calling It Rain
8	Cro Cro	Icons	Pious Poor But Proud	Goodness Delayed
9	Skatie	Revue	Calypso Woman	Jack And Jill

Place	Artiste	Tent	Song 1	Song 2
10	The Incredible Myron B	Kaiso Karavan	One More Sip	First Black Prime Minister
11	Pink Panther	Revue	De Richest Man	Not Tonight
12	Bodyguard	Icons	Aloes Vendor	False Papers

The Prizes: 1st – $1,000,000, **2nd** – 500,000, **3rd** – $250,000, **4th** – $150,000, **5th** – $100,000, **6th** to **12th** – $60,000.

The Incredible Myron B was a first-time National Calypso Monarch finalist in 2014. He holds the distinction of having scored a hat-trick of wins (2012, 2013 and 2014) at the National Humor Calypso Monarch Competition. He was also victorious in 2002 and 2004. In 2015 he placed second behind Brother Ebony singing "Ebola Scare" and "Bacchannal Bachannal". Ebony won with "Sign Language" and "My Wife". The Incredible Myron B is also, to date, a four-time National Extempo Monarch finalist. 2007, 2012, 2013 and 2015

In 2014 the Trinbago Unified Calypsonians Organisation (TUCO) along with the general calypso fraternity celebrated one hundred years of vocal calypso recordings. The staging of the 2014 National Calypso Monarch Competition formed part of the celebration.

> The event, celebrating 100 years of vocal calypso recordings, was formatted in three movements. The first, titled The Opening, featured a medley of calypsoes from various eras performed by The Lydian Singers and other vocalists. The second, Water & Fire, was a "shoot-out" between two DJs, featuring popular calypsos [sic] spanning 100 years. The final movement consisted of road marches through the years, and established the connection between calypso, steelband and the masquerade. Making guest appearances were the Mighty Sparrow (Dr. Slinger Francisco), Natasha Wilson, Aaron Duncan and 2014 Junior Calypso Monarch Ronaldo London.
> **[Trinidad Guardian 4 March 2014]**

A People's Choice category was introduced in 2014 as an added incentive for the national calypso monarch finalists. The winner is decided by a count of votes texted in by fans both at home and abroad. At this inaugural People's Choice tally Brian London emerged as the winner, walking away $100,000 richer. A few days earlier, on Thursday 26th February, London won his first National Extempo Monarch title at TUCO's Kaisorama held at the National Academy for the Performing Arts in Port of Spain. His prize at this competition was $150,000. Two days before his Extempo victory his nephew Ronaldo London was crowned National Junior Calypso Monarch 2014 at the Queen's Park Savannah, Brian was among those cheering on the young bard who represented the Fyzabad Secondary School. Ronaldo's winning calypso is titled "Hear My Cry".

In the categories competition at Kaisorama the results are as follows:

Political Commentary:
   1st Mr. Shak – Bois ($25,000)
   2nd Bunny B – Milk ($15,000)
   3rd Brian London – Call Dem Out ($10,000)

Social Commentary:
   1st Kurt Allen – Sweet Sizzling Summer ($25,000)
   2nd Heather Mac Intosh – Nutten Eh Good ($15, 000)
   3rd Leslie Ann Ellis – Blessed With Beauty ($10,000)

Bodyguard (Roger Mohammed) came in for heavy criticism from interesting quarters for his song "False Papers". Loudest among the voices of disapproval was that of none other than veteran calypsonian and former National Calypso Monarch, Sugar Aloes, who himself is well known for his biting political lyrics. In his capacity as manager of the Kalypso Revue Calypso Tent, however, he objected strongly to Bodyguard's performance of the song, labeling it as offensive.

> Osuna [sic] had found the song, "False Papers", offensive and an attack on East Indians. The song is about persons of East Indian descent with false degrees. Osuna [sic], a former monarch who has been criticized in the past for stinging political commentaries also deemed to be anti-Indian and racist, defended his decision saying he had to be mindful of how patrons of the tent he runs at SWWTU Hall, Port-of-Spain felt about the songs his cast sang.
>
> Undeterred from performing his song, Mohammed, a policeman, found a space among the cast of the Icons Calypso Tent, at Ambassador Hotel, St. James, led by another former monarch, Weston "Cro Cro" Rawlins, who also has a reputation for biting political commentaries. He was among those who took Osuna [sic] to task for turning down Mohammed....
>
> Mohammed said the song received a lot of support from the national community, even from persons of East Indian descent. However he noted that there would be people for the song, and others would only hear the word "Indian" and object to it.
>
> "It's just a factual song. I would have to be foolish to cast aspersions on all people of East Indian descent where this is concerned. The song specifically deals with those who have been caught with false CVs, most of whom happen to be people of East Indian descent," he said.

[Newsday 18 February 2014]

These are the lyrics of the first verse and chorus of False Papers:

It easy to say Sat will be Sat
And try to ignore people like that
But Sat Maharaj controls a large group in society
So when he makes a definitive declaration
It carries a lot ah clout
He feel he know what he talking 'bout
But time has a way of recycling the things we say
And holding them up against logic and reason
So when Sat say Indian children beating book while black children beating pan
No cousin, is better you didn't say nutten

'Cause recently one set ah Indian people get caught
With false papers, false papers
I'm yet to see one single African in the lot
And not one ah them fraudsters ever face a court
So your theory have more holes than a water can
Like is better some ah them Indian did beat a pan
When you feel they was beating more book than the African
They was fabricating degrees, defrauding the land

Bodyguard's "Aloes Vendor" was a newly composed song for his final night performance, seemingly inspired by the actions of his former calypso tent manager. *Photo provided by TriniSoca.com*

2015

Date: Sunday 15th February
Venue: Queen's Park Savannah, Port of Spain, Trinidad & Tobago

Order of Appearance

	Artiste	Given Name
1	Queen Victoria	Victoria Cooper
2	Karene Asche	Karene Asche
3	Heather Mac Intosh	Heather Mac Intosh
4	The Incredible Myron B	Myron Bruce
5	Devon Seale	Devon Seale
6	Bunny B	Neville Brown
7	Brian London	Brian London
8	The Original De Fosto Himself	Winston Scarborough
9	Duane O'Connor	Duane O'Connor
10	Chucky	Roderick Gordon
11	Tigress	Joanne Rowley
12	Mistah Shak	Selvon Noel

Results

Place	Artiste	Tent	Song 1	Song 2
1	Chucky	Kaiso House	The Rose	I Believe
2	Devon Seale	Kalypso Revue	My Humble Plea	Soul Judges
3	Karene Asche	Kaiso House	Bridge The Gap	Every Knee Shall Bow
4	Heather Mac Intosh	Icons	Ah Gone	An Ode To 4
5	Mistah Shak	Kaiso House	Pretender's Reminder	Target
6	Brian London	Kalypso Revue	Wishful	Who Vex Loss
7	Duane O'Connor	Kaiso House	Citizen's Pride	Dance Of Deliverance
8	The Incredible Myron B	Kaiso Karavan	Data Analysis	Ebola Scare

Place	Artiste	Tent	Song 1	Song 2
9	Tigress	Kalypso Revue	What You Willing To Die For	Peace Chant
10	Queen Victoria	Kaiso Showkase	Venting	Long Live Calypso
11	Bunny B	Kaiso House	Multi Crisis	Tame Tame Tame
12	The Original De Fosto Himself	Kaiso Karavan	Games	Message Of Patriarchs

The Prizes: 1st – $1,000,000, **2nd** – 500,000, **3rd** – $250,000, **4th** - $150,000, **5th** -$100,000, **6th** to **12th** - $60,000

Bunny B was a first-time National Calypso Monarch finalist in 2015. He was also a finalist in the National Humor Calypso Monarch Competition placing third behind Brother Ebony and The Incredible Myron B. This post-carnival competition was held on Saturday 11th April at the Queen's Park Savannah. Bunny B sang "Tame Tame Tame" and "Old Party Singers".

The Incredible Myron B and Brian London were Extempo finalists at TUCO's Kaisorama – The Night of Champions, held at the Queen's Park Savannah on Thursday 12th February. Myron B placed 2nd earning the $150,000 prize for his efforts while London, who won the competition in 2014, secured 3rd place and the $75,000 prize. The winner was Lingo; his $250,000 prize is the biggest in the history of the Extempo competition.

In 2015 a new Nation Building category was added to the lineup of competitions on TUCO's Kaisorama - Night of Champions. Karene Asche sang "Every Knee Shall Bow" and etched her name as the first winner of that category. The full results of the Categories Finals are as follows:

Nation Building:
- 1st Karene Asche - Every Knee Shall Bow ($50,000)
- 2nd Kurt Allen - Selfie T & T ($30,000)
- 3rd Brian London - Wishful ($20,000)

Political Commentary:
- 1st Devon Seale – My Humble Plea ($50,000)
- 2nd Kurt Allen – King #2 ($30,000)
- 3rd Alicia Richards – Suits For Sale ($20,000)

Social Commentary:
- 1st Heather Mac Intosh – Ah Gone ($50,000)
- 2nd Arnold Jordan – Dis Is My Life ($30,000)
- 3rd The Messenger – The Voice ($20,000)

Two days prior to his second consecutive win on calypso's biggest stage Chucky appeared as a finalist on Fantastic Friday at the Groovy Soca Monarch Competition singing his soca hit "Doh Take It On".

2016

Date: Sunday 7th February
Venue: Queen's Park Savannah, Port of Spain, Trinidad & Tobago

Order of Appearance

	Artiste	Given Name
1	Lady Adanna	Marsha Davis-Clifton
2	Queen Victoria	Victoria Cooper
3	Chalkdust	Dr. Hollis Liverpool
4	Karene Asche	Karene Asche
5	Gypsy	Winston Peters
6	Skatie	Carlos James
7	Mistah Shak	Selvon Noel
8	Cro Cro	Weston Rawlins
9	Devon Seale	Devon Seale
10	Heather Mac Intosh	Heather Mac Intosh
11	Helon Francis	Helon Francis
12	Chuck Gordon	Roderick Gordon

Results

Place	Artiste	Tent	Song 1	Song 2
1	Devon Seale	Kalypso Revue	Respect God's Voice	Spirit Of Carnival
2	Helon Francis	*Unattached*	Paradise	Real Bandits
3	Chuck Gordon	Kaiso House	Fixing Time	It Eh Go Wuk
4	Karene Asche	Kaiso House	Bring Back The Love	De Politics Of Spite
5	Mistah Shak	Kaiso House	Generation Next	#H.Y.S.M.
6	Chalkdust	Kalypso Revue	The Road Bad	When Trini Get Vex
7	Heather Mac Intosh	Icons	By Other Men's Faults	The Headquarters

Place	Artiste	Tent	Song 1	Song 2
8	Queen Victoria	Kaiso Showkase	More Hope	The After Shock
9	Gypsy	Kaiso House	Too Many	Ship Of State
10	Cro Cro	Icons	Advice To D Boss	Ah Feel It For Gayle
11	Skatie	Kalypso Revue	Jus Come Chinee	Back On Track
12	Lady Adanna	Kaiso Showkase	Murder A Day	My Music

The Prizes: 1st – $1,000,000, **2nd** – 500,000, **3rd** – $250,000, **4th** - $150,000, **5th** - $100,000, **6th** to **12th** - $60,000

Victory came for Devon Seale on his ninth trip to the National Calypso Monarch Finals. On two other occasions, in 2001 and 2002, he stood on the sideline as a first reserve. Seale and second-placed Helon Francis are first cousins. They have followed in the calypso footsteps of their aunt Singing Sonia who is the sister of Devon's mother and Helon's father. Singing Sonia was a National Calypso Monarch finalist in 1992, she sang "Are We Us" and "Professional Advice". She placed 8th.

Two weeks before the National Calypso Finals Helon Francis emerged triumphant from a field of 21 finalists at the National Action Cultural Committee's (NACC) Young Kings Calypso Monarch Competition which was also staged at the Grand Stand, Queen's Park Savannah. This was his third attempt at the Young Kings title; he sang "Real Bandits", walking away $100,000 richer. Although listed as unattached during the carnival season, he has been a cast member of the Barrack Yard Tent Experience (The BYTE) since its inception in 2015. The BYTE was officially launched on Wednesday 12th November 2014. In 2016 their "season" ran from February 10th to 28th.

> The self-proclaimed "Last Badjohn of Calypso", Kurt Allen is using "The Barracky [sic] Yard Experience" to bring Trinidad and Tobago … a new concept in the calypso tent….
>
> BYTE is a production of the organisations known as The House of the Badjohns and The Office of the Calypso Monarch headed by "Black Stalin" (Dr Leroy Calliste) and Allen. It is a new, innovative and revolutionary entertainment product that represents the evolution of the traditional calypso tent. The members and cast of BYTE have been in the business for over 50 years collectively. Currently the cast is made up of active members who provide a variety of services….
>
> Patrons at the Barrack Yard Tent Experience can expect a communal barrackyard setting reminiscent of the 1900s. Social conscious lyrics, melodies, vibrant rhythms, Caribbean fashions and interactive set designs. BYTE will also appeal to the all senses by offering patrons authentic barrackyard food. **[Sunday Express 23 November 2014]**

Helon Francis was a first-time finalist at the National Calypso Monarch Competition in 2016.

Lady Adanna was also a first-time National Calypso Monarch finalist in 2016. A few weeks earlier, on January 18th, she placed third among a field of twenty at the National Women's Action Committee's (NWAC) 32nd Annual National Calypso Queen Competition held at Queen's Hall in St. Ann's. Singing "Murder A Day" her prize was $40,000. She debuted at this competition in 1994.

In the categories competition at Kaisorama – The Night Of Champions the results are as follows:

Social Commentary:
- 1st Karene Asche – Bring Back The Love ($50,000)
- 2nd Brian London – We Trinidad ($30,000)
- 3rd Helon Francis – Paradise ($20,000)

Political Commentary:
- 1st Duane O'Connor – Modern Nursery Rhymes ($50,000)
- 2nd Cro Cro – Advice To D Boss ($30,000)
- 3rd Chuck Gordon – Fixing Time ($20,000)

The Nation Building Category was discontinued in 2016, one year after its introduction (see page??).

The Extempo component of Kaisorama - The Night Of Champions was won by Gypsy who went up against defending champion Lingo in the final round. Gypsy beat Black Sage and Lingo dismissed Myron B at the semi-final round. Brian London, Dion Diaz, Lady Africa and Abebele were all eliminated at the first round. Kaisorama is staged on the Thursday before the National Calypso Finals on Carnival Sunday night.

Gypsy won $250,000
Lingo won $150,000
Myron B & Black Sage, eliminated at semifinal round, each received $125,000
The others won $20,000 each

It was a close call for Skatie in 2016 as he made his bid for a spot among the finalists at calypso's premier event.

> Three days after being thrown out of the Calypso Fiesta competition, for not paying a one hundred dollar registration fee, calypsonian Carlos "Skatie" James yesterday left the Hall of Justice in Port-of-Spain a happy bard, after a High Court Judge ruled in favour of his injunction against the Trinidad Unified Calypsonians Organisation (TUCO) which paved the way for him performing last night in position 41 at the competition at Skinner Park in San Fernando.

> 'Skatie' filed for judicial review claiming TUCO's decision last Wednesday to bar him from the semi-final round of the National Calypso Monarch Competition (Calypso Fiesta) was unjust and unfair. Presiding Judge, Justice Nadia Kangaloo agreed with him, remarking in his [sic] closing statement that the organisation's decision was "illogical and irrational"....

> TUCO president Lutalo "Bro Resistance" Masimba told Sunday News after the decision, "We are an organisation and we are a members organisation. They decide if we have a competition that you must register for that competition. If you want to be a part of that there must be a registration fee and a date by which you pay that fee.

> "We try not to be too military or draconian in the execution of this rule and that way, members have a lot of leeway to pay the registration fee even as the competitions begin to roll. Someone who did not register, to my mind, would be indicating they do not wish to be part of the competition ... yet the court said our decision was illogical"

[Newsday 31 January 2016]

This was Skatie's twelfth National Calypso Monarch Final; see appendices A (ii) and C (ii).

Mr. Shak emerged triumphant among a field of eight in the Calypso Monarch component of the San Fernando Carnival Committee's Night Of The Sando Monarchs, Pre-Dimanche Gras Show. This was his second Pre-Dimanche Gras calypso victory, his first was in 2012 when he sang "Blueprint". His winning song in 2016 was "Generation Next", his prize was $20,000. Queen Victoria was also among the eight bards vying for the southern title in 2016. She sang "The After Shock" and walked away with the $14,000 second prize. She placed third in 2013 with "D Betrayal" and second in 2014 with "Political Love Affair." The San Fernando Pre-Dimanche Gras Show is staged annually on the Wednesday before Carnival Sunday night.

Appendix A (i)

A Profile of the Placing in the National/International Power Soca Monarch Finals
(Coverage: 1993 – 2016)

3Canal	12th 1999
5 Star Akil	**Finalist 2016
Adrian Clarke	6th 1996
Ajala	9th 1993, 6th 1995, 14th 1997 [Tied with Third Bass], 19th 1999
Ajamo	14th 1996
Alan Welch	*Finalist 1993
All Rounder	6th 1993, *Finalist 1994
Allison Hinds	6th 1998
Andy "Blood" Armstrong	20th 1998 [Tied with Oscar B], 8th 1999, **Finalist 2011
Andy Stevenson	6th 1997, 11th 1998
Ann-G	**Finalist 2014
Anslem Douglas	*Finalist 1993, 5th 1995, 10th 1999, 8th 2000
Baby Killa aka Mr. Killa	14th 2005, **Finalist 2010, 2nd 2014 [Tied with Destra and Iwer], **Finalist 2015
Bally	*Finalist 1993, *Finalist 1994, 11th 1995, 7th 1997
Baron	*Finalist 1993
Barry Chandler	9th 2007
Benjai	15th 2002, 3rd 2013
Benjai & Scarface	7th 2005
Berbice	8th 2009
Bindley B	*Finalist 1993
Blackie	24th 1995, 27th 1998
Blaxx	8th 2002, 17th 2003, 12th 2004, 6th 2005, 6th 2007, 6th 2008, 4th 2009, **Finalist 2010, 4th 2012 [Tied with Prophet Benjamin], **Finalist 2015, 3rd 2016 [Tied with Patrice Roberts]
Blazer	7th 2003, 5th 2004
Blueboy aka Super Blue	1st 1993, 1st 1994, 2nd 1995, 1st 1996, 1st 1997 [Tied with Ronnie Mc Intosh], 1st 1998, 3rd 1999, 1st 2000, 5th 2001, 11th 2002, 1st 2013 [Tied with Machel Montano], **Finalist 2014
Brother Marvin	16th 1996
Brother Resistance	25th 1998 [Tied with Lady Spencer], 14th 1999
Bunji Garlin	22nd 1999, 6th 2000, 2nd 2001, 1st 2002 [Tied with Iwer George], 2nd 2003, 1st 2004, 1st 2005, 2nd 2006, 1st 2008, 2nd 2009 [Tied with Iwer George], 3rd 2011

A Profile of the Placing in the National/International Power Soca Monarch Finals (Coverage: 1993 – 2016)

Byke	25th 1999
Candi Hoyte	23rd 2000
Celtic Invasion	17th 2002
Chinese Laundry	10th 1997, 13th 1998, 7th 1999, 12th 2000
Choko	17th 1997
Chris Garcia	9th 1996
Claudette Peters	11th 2009
Cloud 5	**Finalist 2016
Colin Lucas	*Finalist 1993, *Finalist 1994, 3rd 1995, 21st 1997 [Tied with Sprangalang], 12th 1998, 20th 1999
Crazy	5th 1993, *Finalist 1994, 12th 1995, 11th 1996, 18th 1997, 23rd 1998, 11th 1999
Daddy Chess	**Finalist 2010
D'Hitman	12th 2005
De Fosto	7th 1993, *Finalist 1994, 9th 1995, 10th 1996, 7th 1998 [Tied with Tony Prescott]
Denise "Saucy Wow" Belfon	13th 1995, 16th 1998, 14th 2001, 7th 2002, 11th 2003, 4th 2004, 9th 2005, 11th 2007
Denyse Plummer	3rd 1994, 8th 1995, 15th 1996, 8th 1997, 4th 1998, 9th 1999, 16th 2000
Dereck Seales	24th 2000, 8th 2001, 9th 2003, 10th 2005 [Tied with Sean Caruth]
Designer	*Finalist 1993, 17th 1995
Destra	4th 2001, 10th 2002, 3rd 2003, 3rd 2004, **Finalist 2011, 3rd 2012, 4th 2013, 2nd 2014 [Tied with Mr. Killa and Iwer]
Devon George	*Finalist 1994
Devon Matthews	**Finalist 2013, **Finalist 2014
Double D	24th 1997
Dawg E. Slaughter (AKA Mr Slaughter)	10th 2007
Drupatee	8th 1993
Edwin Charles	5th 2000
Edwin Yearwood	3rd 1997
Ella Andall	*Finalist 1994
Erphaan Alves	**Finalist 2012
Errol Asche	*Finalist 1994
Exposer	*Finalist 1993
Farmer Nappy	11th 2001, **Finalist 2010, **Finalist 2016
Fay Ann Lyons	14th 2002, 4th 2003, 14th 2004, 4th 2005, 7th 2006, 8th 2007, 3rd 2008, 1st 2009, 2nd 2010, 4th 2011
Fireman	**Finalist 2012

A Profile of the Placing in the National/International Power Soca Monarch Finals (Coverage: 1993 – 2016)

Flava	5th 1999
Flo PG	18th 2003, 17th 2004
Fya Empress	**Finalist 2013
General Grant	11th 1997
Ghetto Flex	18th 1999
Gillo	20th 1997
Godfather's Asylum	16th 2003
Godfrey Dublin	13th 2001
Gypsy	3rd 1993, *Finalist 1994
Hard Knoxx	**Finalist 2012
Hypasounds	**Finalist 2016
Impulse	12th 2002
Inspector	23rd 1997
Iwer George	10th 1993, 4th 1994 [Tied with Ronnie Mc Intosh], 10th 1995, 7th 1996 [Tied with Leon Coldero], 5th 1997, 2nd 1998, 2nd 1999, 2nd 2000, 1st 2002 [Tied with Bunji Garlin], 1st 2003, 11th 2004, 3rd 2005, 3rd 2006, 1st 2007, 2nd 2008, 2nd 2009 [Tied with Bunji Garlin], 2nd 2011, 2nd 2012, 2nd 2014 [Tied with Destra and Mr. Killa], 2nd 2015
JW and Blaze	5th 2007, 1st 2010, **Finalist 2011, **Finalist 2013
Jay Dee	21st 2000
Johnny King	*Finalist 1993
Kernal Roberts aka Kitch	**Finalist 2015
Khiomal	10th 2009
KI	**Finalist 2015
Kid Site	25th 1997
KMC	5th 1998, 16th 2002, 5th 2003
KMC & Ronnie McIntosh	**Finalist 2010
Knycky Cordner	8th 2005
Kurt Allen	1st 1999
Lady Spencer	25th 1998 [Tied with Brother Resistance]
Laventille Rhythm Section	22nd 1998
Lennox Picou	*Finalist 1993
Leon Coldero	20th 1995, 7th 1996 [Tied with Iwer George], 9th 1997, 18th 1998, 10th 2001
Lil Bits	**Finalist 2013
Luni Spark & Electrify	11th 2008, 9th 2009

A Profile of the Placing in the National/International Power Soca Monarch Finals (Coverage: 1993 – 2016)

Luta	*Finalist 1994, 15th 1995
Lyrikal	**Finalist 2014, **Finalist 2016
M1 aka Menace	**Finalist 2016
Mac Fingall	5th 1996, 16th 1997
Machel Montano	4th 1993, 6th 1994, 7th 1995, 3rd 1996, 1st 2011, 1st 2012, 1st 2013 [Tied with SuperBlue], 1st 2014, 1st 2015
Marcia Miranda	22nd 1995, 14th 1998, 23rd 1999, 13th 2000
Maximus Dan	13th 2002, 6th 2003
Melanie Hudson	12th 1997 [Tied with Peter Cipriani], 10th 1998
Michael Thompson	17th 1996
Michelle Sylvester	9th 2004
Michelle Xavier	**Finalist 2011
Mikey	**Finalist 2012
Minmi	12th 2007
Miss Alysha	8th 2006
Mr. Patch	11th 2000
Mr. Starr	15th 2005
Nadia Batson	4th 2006, 2nd 2007, 4th 2008, **Finalist 2012, **Finalist 2014
Nadia Batson & Patrice Roberts	**Finalist 2011
Naya George	3rd 2002, 12th 2003
Nicole Greaves	25th 2000
Nigel Lewis	2nd 1996, 19th 1997, 10th 2000
Nikki Crosby aka Granny	15th 1998, 3rd 2015
Nnika	9th 2008 [Tied with Pelf]
Olatunji Yearwood	7th 2007, **Finalist 2016
Onika Bostic	4th 2002, 8th 2004
Oscar B	4th 1997, 20th 1998 [Tied with Andy Armstrong]
Patrice Roberts	13th 2003, 20th 2004, 5th 2005, 4th 2007, 7th 2009, **Finalist 2014, **Finalist 2015, 3rd 2016 [Tied with Blaxx]
Pelf	9th 2008 [Tied with Nnika]
Peter C. Lewis	19th 1998, 3rd 2001
Peter Cipriani	14th 1995, 12th 1997 [Tied with Melanie Hudson]
Peter Ram	**Finalist 2016
Poser	*Finalist 1994
Preacher	*Finalist 1993, 2nd 1994, 19th 1995, 13th 1996, 28th 1998, 19th 2000

A Profile of the Placing in the National/International Power Soca Monarch Finals (Coverage: 1993 – 2016)

Precious	14th 2000
Preedy	2nd 2016
Prince Unique	*Finalist 1993, 23rd 1995
Problem Child	8th 2008
Prophet Benjamin	4th 2012 [Tied with Blaxx]
Protector	*Finalist 1994
Pternsky	**Finalist 2016
Ravi B	**Finalist 2011
Red Plastic Bag	4th 2000
Remo	6th 1999
Revealer	*Finalist 1993
Ricardo Drue	**Finalist 2016
Ricky T	7th 2008, 12th 2009
Rikki Jai	*Finalist 1993, 16th 1995, 9th 2001, 16th 2004, **Finalist 2016
Rita Jones	5th 2006
Rocky & Ghetto Flex	6th 2002
Roger George	5th 2002
Ronnie McIntosh	2nd 1993, 4th 1994 [Tied with Iwer George], 1st 1995, 4th 1996, 1st 1997 [Tied with Super Blue]
Rootsman	*Finalist 1993, 22nd 2000
Roy Cape	9th 1998
Rupee	6th 2001, 9th 2002, 19th 2003
Sanell Dempster	4th 1999, 11th 2006
Sean Caruth	9th 2000, 7th 2001, 10th 2003, 13th 2004, 10th 2005 [Tied with Dereck Seales]
Sekon Sta aka Nesta Boxhill	**Finalist 2016
Shadow	*Finalist 1993, 21st 1995, 1st 2001
Shal Marshall	**Finalist 2011, **Finalist 2016
Shal Marshall & Screws	3rd 2010
Shammi	14th 2003
Shanaqua	17th 1998
Sheldon Douglas	9th 2006
Shirlane Hendrickson	24th 1999, 17th 2000
Shurwayne Winchester	17th 1999, 20th 2000, 12th 2001, 8th 2003, 2nd 2004, 2nd 2005, 1st 2006, 3rd 2007, 5th 2008, 6th 2009, **Finalist 2012, **Finalist 2013, 4th 2015, **Finalist 2016
Singing Sonia	*Finalist 1993, 22nd 2004

A Profile of the Placing in the National/International Power Soca Monarch Finals (Coverage: 1993 – 2016)

Skinny Fabulous	5th 2009, **Finalist 2010, **Finalist 2011
Snakey	**Finalist 2014, **Finalist 2015
Soca Elvis	6th 2004, 13th 2005
Sonny Mann	*Finalist 1996
Spongy	15th 2004
Sprangalang	21st 1997 [Tied with Colin Lucas]
Squeeze Head & Shal Marshall	**Finalist 2015
Star Child	21st 1999
Steve Sealy	4th 1995, 12th 1996, 16th 1999
Super Jigga TC aka Jaiga TC	**Finalist 2010
Swappi	**Finalist 2012, **Finalist 2013
Tallpree	3rd 2000, 15th 2001, 18th 2002, 21st 2004, 4th 2010, **Finalist 2011, **Finalist 2013
Teddyson John	**Finalist 2016
Terencia (TC) Coward	18th 2000
Terry Seales	10th 2004, 17th 2005, 10th 2006
Third Bass	14th 1997 [Tied with Ajala], **Finalist 2016
Tian Winter	**Finalist 2010, **Finalist 2011
Timmy	7th 2004, 16th 2005
Tony Prescott	7th 1998 [Tied with De Fosto], 13th 1999, 7th 2000, 21st 2003
Tracker	18th 1995
Trini	*Finalist 1994
Trinidad Bill	24th 1998
United Sisters	*Finalist 1993, *Finalist 1994
Victorio	*Finalist 1994
Voice	1st 2016
Vybe aka Mista Vybe	26th 1999, 6th 2006
Vybe & Keisha Stewart	15th 2000
Wanski	15th 2003, 18th 2004
Wayne Rodriguez	3rd 1998, 15th 1999
Wayne T and Silky Slim	*Finalist 1993
Young Marcel	20th 2003, 19th 2004

* No records of placing found   ** Placing withheld by the competition's administrators

Appendix A (ii)

A Profile of the Placing in the National Calypso King/Monarch Finals (Coverage: 1939, and 1953 - 2016)

Abbi Blackman	9th 1992
Alana Sinnette-Khan	8th 2013, 7th 2014
All Rounder	4th 1984, 12th 1998, 14th 2009, 14th 2010
Atilla The Hun	2nd 1939
Baker	5th 1967, 7th 1968
Bally	4th 1987, 7th 1988, 8th 1989, 16th 2009
Baron	3rd 1971, 6th 1984, 9th 1989, 5th 1993 [tied with Gypsy], 4th 1994
Benjai	12th 2011
Black Sage	15th 2007
Black Stalin	4th 1967, 2nd 1969, 4th 1972, 1st 1979, 6th 1980, 3rd 1981, 6th 1982, 2nd 1983, 1st 1985, 2nd 1986, 1st 1987, 3rd 1988, 1st 1991, 6th 1992 [tied with Singing Sandra], 1st 1995, 10th 1996, 4th 1997, 6th 1999
Blakie	*Finalist 1954, 2nd 1959, *Finalist 1960, 7th 1962, 5th 1963, 5th 1964, 7th 1965, 6th 1971, 6th 1973, 7th 1976.
BlueBoy aka Super Blue	6th 1981, 3rd 1983, 3rd 1984, 8th 1985, 8th 1990, 5th 1991, 7th 1993, 11th 1994
Bodyguard	12th 2005, 12th 2014
Bomber	4th 1963, 1st 1964, 2nd 1965 [tied with Terror], 5th 1966, 5th 1974, 4th 1976, 5th 1980, 10th 2002, 6th 2003
Brian London	2nd 2004, 10th 2005, 6th 2006, 8th 2008 [Tied with Kurt Allen], 4th 2009, 2nd 2010, 7th 2011, 9th 2012, 5th 2014, 6th 2015
Brother Marvin	2nd 1996
Brother Mudada	2nd 1976, 8th 1977, 7th 1978, 8th 2005, 5th 2006
Bunny B	11th 2015
Buzzing Bee	9th 1977
Calypso Rose	5th 1968, 3rd 1975, 6th 1977, 1st 1978
Caresser	*Finalist 1939
Caruso	*Finalist 1959
Chalkdust	3rd 1968, 3rd 1969, 3rd 1970, 4th 1971, 5th 1972, 2nd 1973, 6th 1974, 1st 1976, 1st 1977, 5th 1978, 1st 1981, 7th 1982, 5th 1983 [tied with Scrunter], 5th 1984, 4th 1986, 5th 1987, 1st 1989, 6th 1990, 5th 1992, 1st 1993, 3rd 1994, 6th 1996, 9th 1999, 8th 2000, 6th 2001, 2nd 2002, 2nd 2003, 1st 2004, 1st 2005, 3rd 2006, 5th 2007, 5th 2008, 1st 2009, 6th 2010, 3rd 2011, 6th 2012, 9th 2013, 4th 2014, 6th 2016
Commander	*Finalist 1959
Composer	2nd 1964, 6th 1965, 2nd 1967, 2nd 1970, 7th 1974, 4th 1975, 3rd 1976

A Profile of the Placing in the National Calypso King/ Monarch Finals (Coverage: 1939, and 1953 - 2016)

Conqueror	3rd 1966
Contender	15th 2009
Crazy	2nd 1978, 4th 1979, 9th 1983, 8th 1984, 11th 1996, 7th 2000, 8th 2001, 9th 2006, 13th 2007 [Tied with Valentino], 12th 2008 [Tied with Versatile]
Crepesole	4th 1970
Christo aka Cristo	*Finalist 1960, *Finalist 1961, 3rd 1962, 6th 1963, 2nd 1966
Cro Cro	8th 1978, 1st 1988, 2nd 1989, 1st 1990, 2nd 1991, 2nd 1992, 4th 1993, 5th 1994, 2nd 1995, 1st 1996, 2nd 1997, 8th 1998, 2nd 2005, 1st 2007, 2nd 2008, 13th 2009, 11th 2011, 12th 2012, 8th 2014, 10th 2016
Cypher	*Finalist 1956, 1st 1967, 6th 1968
David Rudder	1st 1986, 2nd 1987
De Fosto	6th 1994, 5th 1999, 2nd 2000, 4th 2001, 7th 2002, 3rd 2004, 5th 2005, 10th 2006, 2nd 2007, 3rd 2009, 3rd 2010, 12th 2015
Delamo	8th 1987, 1st 1994 [tied with Luta], 5th 1995, 7th 1996, 7th 1998, 11th 2005
Denyse Plummer	6th 1988, 5th 1989, 7th 1991, 6th 1998, 10th 2000, 1st 2001, 3rd 2002
Designer	8th 1982, 7th 1983, 10th 1992
Devon Seale	8th 1999, 5th 2003, 9th 2005, 3rd 2007, 12th 2010, 4th 2011, 4th 2012, 2nd 2015, 1st 2016
Dictator	*Finalist 1955
Dougla	1st 1961, 8th 1962, 3rd 1963
Duane O'Connor	6th 2007, 1st 2012, 7th 2013, 7th 2015
Duke	1st 1968, 1st 1969, 1st 1970, 1st 1971, 7th 1972, 6th 1976, 7th 1977, 9th 1980, 7th 1981, 4th 1982, 6th 1986, 9th 1995 [tied with Gypsy], 11th 1999, 12th 2001.
Eastlyn Orr	2nd 1990 [tied with Tambu and Kenny J]
Eisenhower	*Finalist 1956
Ella Andall	9th 1996, 11th 1997
Eunice Peters	6th 2013
Explainer	5th 1977, 6th 1978, 3rd 1979, 7th 1980, 8th 1981, 2nd 1982, 8th 1983, 7th 1984, 11th 1998
Funny	5th 1970
GB	10th 1997
Growling Tiger	1st 1939, *Finalist 1959, *Finalist 1960
Gypsy	5th 1985, 3rd 1986, 3rd 1987, 2nd 1988, 5th 1993 [tied with Baron], 9th 1995 [tied with Duke], 1st 1997, 4th 1998, 3rd 1999, 5th 2000, 9th 2002, 8th 2009, 9th 2016
Heather Mac Intosh	11th 2001, 8th 2002, 4th 2003, 8th 2004, 9th 2007, 5th 2012, 3rd 2013, 4th 2015, 7th 2016
Helon Francis	2nd 2016
Hollis Wright	6th 1995, 10th 1999, 6th 2000

A Profile of the Placing in the National Calypso King/Monarch Finals (Coverage: 1939, and 1953 - 2016)

Jervae Caesar	12th 2007
Johnny King	2nd 1984, 6th 1985, 7th 1986
Karene Asche	7th 2006, 3rd 2008, 10th 2009, 1st 2011, 3rd 2012, 5th 2013, 3rd 2015, 4th 2016
Kenny J	4th 1989, 2nd 1990 [tied with Tambu and Eastlyn Orr], 10th 1993, 10th 2001
Kerwin Du Bois	3rd 1996, 5th 1997
King Austin	2nd 1980, 5th 1981, 4th 1983
King Fighter	*Finalist 1957
Kitchener	2nd 1963, 3rd 1964 [tied with Sparrow], 2nd 1971, 2nd 1972, 2nd 1974 [tied with Shadow], 1st 1975
Kizzie Ruiz	10th 2004, 5th 2009, 4th 2010, 9th 2011, 10th 2013
Kurt Allen	9th 1994, 4th 1995, 6th 1997, 8th 2008 [Tied with Brian London], 1st 2010, 6th 2011, 2nd 2012, 2nd 2013, 2nd 2014
Lady Adanna	12th 2016
Leslie Ann Ellis	6th 2005, 7th 2008, 11th 2012
Leveller	6th 1966
Lion	*Finalist 1958
Luta	2nd 1985, 1st 1994 [tied with Delamo], 11th 1995, 12th 1996, 10th 1998, 9th 2001, 5th 2002, 11th 2004, 1st 2006
M'ba	3rd 1993, 7th 1995
Machel Montano	5th 1986, 3rd 1991
Maestro	7th 1973, 8th 1976, 3rd 1977
Maria Bhola	4th 2007
Marvelous Marva	11th 2013
Melody	4th 1953, 1st 1954, *Finalist 1955, *Finalist 1956, 2nd 1958, 2nd 1960, 6th 1967
Merchant	4th 1978, 3rd 1985.
Mistah Shak	7th 2010, 3rd 2014, 5th 2015, 5th 2016
Mystic Prowler	1st 1998, 4th 1999, 10th 2003
Nap Hepburn	3rd 1959, 2nd 1962, 7th 1963, 6th 1964.
Nicole Greaves	8th 2010
Princess Natasha	6th 1987
Panther	3rd 1953, *Finalist 1954, *Finalist 1955
Penguin	3rd 1982, 1st 1984, 4th 1985
Pink Panther	5th 1998, 7th 1999, 9th 2000, 1st 2013, 11th 2014
Poser	7th 1979
Power	4th 1965, 6th 1969, 6th 1970, 7th 1975

A Profile of the Placing in the National Calypso King/ Monarch Finals (Coverage: 1939, and 1953 - 2016)

Pretender	3rd 1939, *Finalist 1954, *Finalist 1955, 1st 1957, *Finalist 1958, *Finalist 1959, 4th 1961, 5th 1969, 8th 1972
Protector	4th 1988, 6th 1989, 8th 1996, 12th 2004, 14th 2010
Psycho	7th 1969
Queen Victoria	12th 2013, 6th 2014, 10th 2015, 8th 2016
Ras Kassa	* Finalist 1939
Ras Kommanda	12th 1999, 9th 2004
Relator	6th 1972, 2nd 1979, 1st 1980, 2nd 1981
Rikki Jai	7th 2001
Roderick Gordon aka Mr. Chucky aka Chuck Gordon	8th 2006, 5th 2010, 4th 2013, 1st 2014, 1st 2015, 3rd 2016
Roger George	8th 2003
Ronnie McIntosh	7th 1997 [tied with Sugar Aloes]
Sad Sack	7th 1970
Scrunter	3rd 1980, 9th 1981, 1st 1982, 5th 1983 [tied with Chalkdust], 8th 1986, 7th 1987
Sean Daniel	7th 2007, 9th 2010
Sekon Alves	15th 2008
Shadow	2nd 1974 [tied with Kitchener], 6th 1975, 5th 1976, 8th 1993, 1st 2000, 2nd 2001, 9th 2003, 6th 2004, 10th 2007
Sheldon Reid	3rd 1998
Short Pants	6th 1979, 11th 1993
Shorty	4th 1968, 4th 1973
Singing Dianne	8th 1974, 5th 1975
Singing Francine	3rd 1972, 3rd 1973, 2nd 1975, 4th 1977, 5th 1979, 4th 1980, 7th 1985, 14th 2008
Singing Sandra	6th 1992 [tied with Stalin], 1st 1999, 3rd 2000, 5th 2001, 4th 2002, 1st 2003, 4th 2004, 3rd 2005, 2nd 2006, 11th 2007, 10th 2008, 6th 2009, 10th 2010, 10th 2012
Singing Sonia	8th 1992
Sir Galba	* Finalist 1954
Skatie	11th 2000, 6th 2002, 3rd 2003, 5th 2004, 7th 2005, 4th 2006, 8th 2007, 11th 2008, 12th 2009, 12th 2010, 9th 2014, 11th 2016
Skipper	2nd 1958, *Finalist 1961
Small Island Pride	2nd 1953, 2nd 1955, *Finalist 1956, *Finalist 1960
Sniper	1st 1965, 2nd 1968

A Profile of the Placing in the National Calypso King/Monarch Finals (Coverage: 1939, and 1953 - 2016)

Sparrow	1st 1956, 1st 1960, 2nd 1961, 1st 1962, 1st 1963, 3rd 1964 [tied with Kitchener], 1st 1972, 1st 1973, 1st 1974, 1st 1992, 2nd 1993, 3rd 1995
Spitfire	*Finalist 1955, *Finalist 1957
Spoiler	1st 1953, * Finalist 1954, 1st 1955, 2nd 1957, * Finalist 1959, *Finalist 1960
Stinger	7th 1994, 12th 2000, 12th 2006, 4th 2008, 11th 2009, 5th 2011, 8th 2012
Striker	3rd 1957, 1st 1958, 1st 1959, 3rd 1960, *Finalist 1961
Sugar Aloes	7th 1989, 5th 1990, 6th 1991, 3rd 1992, 9th 1993, 8th 1995, 5th 1996, 7th 1997 [tied with Ronnie McIntosh], 2nd 1998, 2nd 1999, 4th 2000, 3rd 2001, 1st 2002, 7th 2003, 7th 2004, 4th 2005, 11th 2006, 1st 2008, 7th 2009, 2nd 2011, 7th 2012
Superior	* Finalist 1958, 6th 1962, 8th 1970, 7th 1971, 4th 1974
Syncopator	* Finalist 1956
Tambu	8th 1988, 3rd 1989, 2nd 1990 [tied with Kenny J and Eastlyn Orr], 8th 1991
Tameka Darius	8th 2011
Taylor	6th 2008
Terror	2nd 1965 [tied with Bomber], 1st 1966, 7th 1967, 3rd 1978
The Incredible Myron B	10th 2014, 8th 2015
Tigress	5th 1988, 4th 1996, 9th 1997, 2nd 2009, 10th 2011, 9th 2015
Tiny Terror	*Finalist 1958
Tobago Crusoe/Crusoe Kid	5th 1973, 2nd 1977, 8th 1980, 4th 1981, 5th 1982, 1st 1983
Trini	8th 1994
Twiggy	9th 2009, 11th 2010
Valentino	5th 1971, 8th 1979, 13th 2007 [Tied with Crazy]
Versatile	12th 2008 [Tied with Crazy]
Watchman	7th 1990, 4th 1991, 4th 1992, 10th 1994, 3rd 1997
Wayne Rodriguez	9th 1998.
Wrangler	*Finalist 1958
Young Creole/King Creole	5th 1962, 4th 1969
Young Killer	*Finalist 1957, 4th 1962, 7th 1964, 5th 1965, 4th 1966, 3rd 1967
Yul Brynner aka Bryner	*Finalist 1960, 3rd 1961.
Ziegfeld	*Finalist 1939.

* No records of placing found

Appendix A (iii)

A Profile of the Placing in the Groovy Soca Monarch Finals (Coverage: 2005 - 2015)

5 Star Akil	**Finalist 2015
Ainsley King	**Finalist 2010
All Rounder	**Finalist 2011
Benjai	3rd 2009, 2nd 2011, 3rd 2012, **Finalist 2013, **Finalist 2015
Biggie Irie	1st 2007, 9th 2008, 5th 2009, **Finalist 2014
Blackie	3rd 2005, 8th 2007
Blaxx	4th 2011, **Finalist 2012, 3rd 2013, **Finalist 2015
Blazer Dan aka Blazer	9th 2007
Cassi	**Finalist 2011, **Finalist 2014
Chow Chow	**Finalist 2015
Chucky aka Mr. Chucky aka Chuck Gordon	3rd 2006, 2nd 2007, **Finalist 2010, **Finalist 2011, **Finalist 2012, **Finalist 2015
Crazy	6th 2007
Denise Belfon	**Finalist 2011, **Finalist 2013, **Finalist 2014
Destra	3rd 2011, **Finalist 2012, **Finalist 2013, 4th 2014, 4th 2015
Drupatee	**Finalist 2013
Erphaan Alves	**Finalist 2012, **Finalist 2014, **Finalist 2015
Fadda Fox	**Finalist 2015
Farmer Nappy	4th 2008, **Finalist 2013, 3rd 2014, 2nd 2015
Fay Ann Lyons-Alvarez	1st 2009, 2nd 2010,
Fireball	10th 2007
H20 Flo	2nd 2005
Hunter	9th 2009
Iwer	2nd 2013
JW & Blaze	**Finalist 2012
Jahmoun	**Finalist 2011
Jamsie P	6th 2005
Johnny King	7th 2005
KI	**Finalist 2012
Kees	1st 2011, 5th 2012

A Profile of the Placing in the Groovy Soca Monarch Finals (Coverage: 2005 - 2015)

Keishea Stewart	5th 2005
Kerwin Du Bois	6th 2009, **Finalist 2011, 2nd 2012, 1st 2014
Kerwin Du Bois & Shal Marshall	3rd 2008
Kerwin Du Bois & Farmer Nappy	**Finalist 2010
KMC	**Finalist 2010
Leadpipe & Saddis	**Finalist 2015
Lil' Bitts	8th 2005, **Finalist 2010
Lyrikal	**Finalist 2015
Machel Montano	1st 2012, 1st 2013, 2nd 2014
Megan Walrond	**Finalist 2011
Metro	**Finalist 2010
Michelle Sylvester	1st 2005, 4th 2006
Mini Priest	4th 2005
Mr. Dale	5th 2008
Mr. Famous	**Finalist 2014
Nadia Batson	3rd 2007, 7th 2009, 4th 2012, **Finalist 2013, **Finalist 2015
Nesta Boxhill aka Sekon Sta	9th 2005
Nnika	11th 2007, **Finalist 2010
OG	11th 2008
Olatunji	1st 2015
Patch & Mastermind	11th 2009
Patrice Roberts	5th 2007, 2nd 2008, 4th 2010, **Finalist 2011, **Finalist 2012, **Finalist 2013
Peter C. Lewis	8th 2008
Ras Star	**Finalist 2011
Ravi B	4th 2013, **Finalist 2014
Ricardo Drue	3rd 2015
Rikki Jai	3rd 2010
Sean Caruth	6th 2006
Shal Marshall	**Finalist 2012
Shurwayne Winchester	1st 2006, 4th 2007, 1st 2008, 2nd 2009, 1st 2010, **Finalist 2011
Skhi	6th 2008
Skinny Fabulous	**Finalist 2014, **Finalist 2015

A Profile of the Placing in the Groovy Soca Monarch Finals
(Coverage: 2005 - 2015)

Super Jigga TC aka Jaiga TC	**Finalist 2012
Surge	5th 2006
Terencia (TC) Coward	**Finalist 2010
Tallpree	**Finalist 2014
Terry Seales	7th 2007
Tizzy	10th 2008
Tizzy & Richard Trumpet	8th 2009
Tony Prescott	7th 2008
Umi Marcano	12th 2007
Yankee Boy and Patch	**Finalist 2011
Zan	10th 2009
Zan and Patrice Roberts	2nd 2006
Zoelah	4th 2009, **Finalist 2010

** Placing withheld by the competition's administrators

Appendix B (i)

Streaks – A Breakdown of Consecutive Appearances in the National/International Power Soca Monarch Finals (Coverage: 1993 - 2016)

The artistes are listed below in order from the longest string of consecutive appearances to the shortest. This pattern is also adopted in cases where an artiste has had more than one streak over the years.

Artiste	Streak
Super Blue	1993 – 2002, 2013 - 2014. This is Super Blue's entire experience in the soca finals.
Fay Ann Lyons-Alvarez	2002 – 2011. This is Fay Ann Lyons's entire experience in the power soca finals.
Iwer George	1993 – 2000, 2002 – 2009. 2011 – 2012
Bunji Garlin	1999 – 2006, 2008 – 2009
Shurwayne Winchester	2003 – 2009, 1999 – 2001, 2012 – 2013, 2015 - 2016.
Crazy	1993 – 1999. This is Crazy's entire experience in the power soca finals
Denyse Plummer	1994 – 2000. This is Denyse Plummer's entire experience in the soca finals.
Machel Montano	2011 – 2015, 1993 – 1996.
Ronnie McIntosh	1993 – 1997.
Denise Belfon	2001 – 2005.
Blaxx	2002 – 2005, 2007 – 2010, 2015 -2016.
De Fosto	1993 – 1996.
Preacher	1993 – 1996.
Leon Coldero	1995 – 1998.
Chinese Laundry	1997 – 2000. This is Chinese Laundry's entire experience in the soca finals.
Destra	2001– 2004, 2011 – 2013.
Colin Lucas	1993 – 1995, 1997 – 1999. This is Colin Lucas's entire experience in the soca finals.
Patrice Roberts	2003 – 2005. 2014 – 2016
Sean Caruth	2003 – 2005, 2000 – 2001. This is Sean Caruth's entire experience in the power soca finals.
Tallpree	2000 – 2002, 2010 – 2011.
Bally	1993 – 1995.
Marcia Miranda	1998 – 2000.
Tony Prescott	1998 – 2000.
Rupee	2001 – 2003. This is Rupee's entire experience in the soca finals.
Terry Seales	2004 – 2006. This is Terry Seales' entire experience in the power soca finals.
Nadia Batson	2006 – 2008.
Skinny Fabulous	2009 – 2011 This is Skinny Fabulous' entire experience in the soca finals.

Streaks – A Breakdown of Consecutive Appearances in the National/International Power Soca Monarch Finals (Coverage: 1993 - 2016)

Artiste	Streak
All Rounder	1993 – 1994. This is All Rounder's entire experience in the power soca finals.
Andy Armstrong	1998 – 1999
JW & Blaze	2010 – 2011
Anslem Douglas	1999 – 2000
Blazer	2003 – 2004. This is Blazer's entire experience in the power soca finals.
Brother Resistance	1998 – 1999. This is Brother Resistance's entire experience in the soca finals.
Dereck Seales	2000 – 2001.
Flo PG	2003 – 2004. This is Flo PG's entire experience in the soca finals.
Gypsy	1993 – 1994. This is Gypsy's entire experience in the soca finals.
KMC	2002 – 2003.
Luta	1994 – 1995. This is Luta's entire experience in the soca finals.
Mac Fingall	1996 – 1997. This is Mac Fingall's entire experience in the soca finals.
Maximus Dan	2002 – 2003. This is Maximus Dan's entire experience in the soca finals.
Melanie Hudson	1997 – 1998. This is Melanie Hudson's entire experience in the soca finals.
Naya George	2002 – 2003. This is Naya George's entire experience in the soca finals.
Nigel Lewis	1996 – 1997.
Shirlane Hendrickson	1999 – 2000. This is Shirlane Hendrickson's entire experience in the soca finals.
Soca Elvis	2004 – 2005. This is Soca Elvis' entire experience in the soca finals.
Steve Sealy	1995 – 1996.
Timmy	2004 – 2005. This is Timmy's entire experience in the soca finals.
United Sisters	1993 – 1994. This is The United Sisters' entire experience in the soca finals.
Wanski	2003 – 2004. This is Wanski's entire experience in the soca finals.
Wayne Rodriguez	1998 – 1999. This is Wayne Rodriguez's entire experience in the soca finals.
Young Marcel	2003 – 2004. This is Young Marcel's entire experience in the soca finals.
Tian Winter	2010 – 2011. This is Tian Winter's entire experience in the soca finals.
Swappi	2012 – 2013 This is Swappi's entire experience in the soca finals
Devon Matthews	2013 – 2014
Baby Killa aka Mr. Killa	2014 – 2015
Snakey	2014 – 2015

Appendix B (ii)

Streaks – A Breakdown of Consecutive Appearances in the National Calypso King/Monarch Finals (Coverage: 1939, and 1953 - 2016)

The artistes are listed below in order from the longest string of consecutive appearances to the shortest. This pattern is also adopted in cases where an artiste has had a number of streaks over the years.

It's important to note here that the profiles for artistes like Sparrow, Kitchener, Melody and Shadow, among others, would have been different had they not boycotted the competition in the years that they did.

Artiste	Streak
Chalkdust	1999 – 2014, 1968 – 1974, 1981 – 1984, 1976 – 1978, 1992 – 1994, 1986 – 1987, 1989 – 1990
Sugar Aloes	1995 – 2006, 1989 – 1993, 2008 – 2009, 2011 – 2012
Singing Sandra	1999 – 2010.
Cro Cro	1988 – 1998, 2007 – 2009, 2011 – 2012
Skatie	2002 – 2010.
Explainer	1977 – 1984.
Black Stalin	1979 – 1983, 1985 – 1988, 1995 – 1997, 1991 – 1992
Duke	1968 – 1972, 1980 – 1982, 1976 – 1977
Sparrow	1960 – 1964, 1972 – 1974, 1992 – 1993
Brian London	2008 – 2012, 2004 – 2006, 2014 - 2015
Kurt Allen	2010 – 2014, 1994 – 1995
Striker	1957 – 1961. This is Striker's entire experience in the national finals.
De Fosto	1999 – 2002, 2004 – 2007, 2009-2010
Gypsy	1985 – 1988, 1997 – 2000.
Heather Mac Intosh	2001 – 2004, 2012 – 2013, 2015 – 2016
Bomber	1963 – 1966, 2002 – 2003
Blakie	1962 – 1965, 1959 – 1960
Scrunter	1980 – 1983, 1986 – 1987. This is Scrunter's entire experience in the national finals.
Melody	1953 – 1956
Christo aka Cristo	1960 – 1963.
Tambu	1988 – 1991. This is Tambu's entire experience in the national finals.

Streaks – A Breakdown of Consecutive Appearances in the National Calypso King/Monarch Finals
(Coverage: 1939, and 1953 - 2016)

Artiste	Streak
Tobago Crusoe aka Crusoe Kid	1980 – 1983
Young Killer	1964 – 1967
Roderick Gordon/Mr. Chucky/ Chuck Gordon	2013 – 2016
Queen Victoria	2013 – 2016
Crazy	2006 – 2008, 1978 – 1979, 1983 – 1984, 2000 – 2001.
Shadow	1974 – 1976, 2000 – 2001, 2003 – 2004.
BlueBoy aka Super Blue	1983 – 1985, 1990 – 1991, 1993 – 1994.
Karene Asche	2011 – 2013, 2008 – 2009, 2015 – 2016
Spoiler	1953 – 1955, 1959 – 1960.
Pretender	1957 – 1959, 1954 – 1955
Brother Mudada	1976 – 1978, 2005 – 2006. This is Brother Mudada's entire experience in the national finals.
Composer	1974 – 1976, 1964 – 1965
Luta	1994 – 1996, 2001 – 2002
Denyse Plummer	2000 – 2002, 1988 – 1989
Pink Panther	1998 – 2000, 2013 – 2014. This is Pink Panther's entire experience in the national finals.
Devon Seale	2010 – 2012, 2015 - 2016
Terror	1965 – 1967.
Panther	1953 – 1955. This is Panther's entire experience in the national finals.
Nap Hepburn	1962 – 1964.
Bally	1987 – 1989.
Dougla	1961 – 1963. This is Dougla's entire experience in the national finals.
Delamo	1994 – 1996
Johnny King	1984 – 1986. This is Johnny King's entire experience in the national finals.
Relator	1979 – 1981.
Watchman	1990 – 1992
Kizzie Ruiz	2009 – 2011
Mistah Shak	2014 – 2016

Streaks – A Breakdown of Consecutive Appearances in the National Calypso King/Monarch Finals
(Coverage: 1939, and 1953 - 2016)

Artiste	Streak
Kitchener	1963 – 1964, 1971 – 1972, 1974 – 1975. This is Kitchener's entire experience in the national finals.
Singing Francine	1972 – 1973, 1979 – 1980.
Stinger	2008 – 2009, 2011 – 2012
Calypso Rose	1977 – 1978
Baker	1967 – 1968. This is Baker's entire experience in the national finals.
Baron	1993 – 1994
Cypher	1967 – 1968.
David Rudder	1986 – 1987. This is David Rudder's entire experience in the national finals.
Designer	1982 – 1983.
Ella Andall	1996 – 1997. This is Ella Andall's entire experience in the national finals.
Hollis Wright	1999 – 2000.
Kenny J	1989 – 1990
Kerwin Du Bois	1996 – 1997. This is Kerwin Du Bois's entire experience in the national finals.
King Austin	1980 – 1981.
Maestro	1976 – 1977.
Penguin	1984 – 1985.
Power	1969 – 1970
Protector	1988 – 1989
Singing Dianne	1974 – 1975. This is Singing Dianne's entire experience in the national finals.
Small Island Pride	1955 – 1956
Superior	1970 – 1971
Growling Tiger	1959 – 1960.
Mystic Prowler	1998 – 1999.
Tigress	1996 – 1997.
Twiggy	2009 – 2010
Yul Brynner aka Bryner	1960 – 1961. This is Bryner's entire experience in the national finals.
Alana Sinnette-Khan	2013 – 2014
Duane O'Connor	2012 – 2013
The Incredible Myron B	2014 – 2015

Appendix B (iii)

Streaks – A Breakdown of Consecutive Appearances in the Groovy Soca Monarch Finals (Coverage: 2005 - 2015)

The artistes are listed below in order from the longest string of consecutive appearances to the shortest. This pattern is also adopted in cases where an artiste has had more than one streak over the years.

Artiste	Streak
Shurwayne Winchester	2006 – 2011
Destra	2011 – 2015
Patrice Roberts	2010 – 2013, 2007 – 2008
Roderick Gordon/Mr. Chucky/Chuck Gordon	2010 – 2012, 2006 – 2007
Biggie Irie	2007 – 2009
Benjai	2011 – 2013
Blaxx	2011 – 2013
Machel Montano	2012 – 2014
Farmer Nappy	2013 – 2015
Michelle Sylvester	2005 – 2006
Fay Ann Lyons-Alvarez	2009 – 2010
Zoelah	2009 – 2010
Kees	2011 – 2012
Kerwin Du Bois	2011 – 2012
Nadia Batson	2012 – 2013
Denise Belfon	2013 – 2014
Ravi B	2013 – 2014
Erphaan Alves	2014 - 2015
Skinny Fabulous	2014 - 2015

Although Kerwin Du Bois enjoys a streak from 2008 to 2012, he was a part of a duo (Kerwin Du Bois & Shal Marshall) in 2008 and (Kerwin Du Bois & Farmer Nappy) in 2010.

Appendix C (i)

A Score Sheet of Appearances in the National/International Power Soca Monarch Finals (Coverage: 1993 - 2016)

Appearances	Artiste
Twenty	Iwer George
Nineteen Appearances	
Eighteen Appearances	
Seventeen Appearances	
Sixteen Appearances	
Fifteen Appearances	
Fourteen Appearances	Shurwayne Winchester
Thirteen Appearances	
Twelve Appearances	Super Blue
Eleven Appearances	Bunji Garlin, Blaxx
Ten Appearances	Fay Ann Lyons-Alvarez
Nine Appearances	Machel Montano
Eight Appearances	Denise Belfon, Destra, Patrice Roberts
Seven Appearances	Denise Plummer, Crazy, Tallpree
Six Appearances	Colin Lucas, Preacher
Five Appearances	De Fosto, Leon Coldero, Sean Caruth, Nadia Batson, Ronnie McIntosh, Rikki Jai
Four Appearances	Ajala, Anslem Douglas, Bally, Chinese Laundry, Dereck Seales, Marcia Miranda, Tony Prescott, JW and Blaze, Baby Killa/Mr. Killa
Three Appearances	Nigel Lewis, Shadow, Steve Sealy, Terry Seales, Rupee, Andy Armstrong, Skinny Fabulous, KMC, Farmer Nappy
Two Appearances	All Rounder, Andy Stephenson, Blackie, Blazer, Flo PG, Luta, Brother Resistance, Designer, Gypsy, Mac Fingall, Maximus Dan, Onika Bostic, Melanie Hudson, Naya George, Oscar B, Sanell Dempster, Shirlane Hendrickson, Peter C. Lewis, Peter Cipriani, Prince Unique, Rootsman, Singing Sonia, Timmy, Soca Elvis, The United Sisters, Vybe/Mista Vybe, Wanski, Wayne Rodriguez, Young Marcel, Ricky T, Tian Winter, Benjai, Devon Matthews, Swappi, Snakey, Nicky Crosby/Granny, Olatunji Yearwood, Third Bass, Luni Spark & Electrify, Shal Marshall, Lyrikal

A Score Sheet of Appearances in the National/International Power Soca Monarch Finals (Coverage: 1993 - 2016)

Appearances	Artiste
One Appearance	3Canal, Adrian Clarke, Ajamu, Alan Welch, Allison Hinds, Byke, Trini, Baron, Benjai and Scarface, Trinidad Bill, Bindley B, Brother Marvin, Remo, Flava, Candi Hoyte, Celtic Invasion, Choko, Chris Garcia, Gillo, Jay Dee, Devon George, Double D, Drupatee, Edwin Charles, Impulse, Edwin Yearwood, Ella Andall, Errol Asche, Exposer, Poser, General Grant, D'Hitman, Ghetto Flex, Rocky and Ghetto Flex, Spongy, Godfather's Asylum, Godfrey Dublin, Johnny King, Kid Site, Knycky Cordner, Kurt Allen, Lady Spencer, Laventille Rhythm Section, Mr. Starr, Lennox Picou, Michael Thompson, Shanaqua, Michele Sylvester, Miss Alysha, Mr. Patch, Inspector, Nicole Greaves, Precious, Protector, Red Plastic Bag, Revealer, Rita Jones, Tracker, Roger George, Minmi, Roy Cape, Shammi, Sheldon Douglas, Sonny Mann, Sprangalang, Star Child, Terencia Coward, Victorio, Vybe & Keisha Stewart, Barry Chandler, Wayne T & Silky Slim, Dawg E. Slaughter (AKA Mr Slaughter), Nnika, Pelf, Problem Child, Daddy Chess, Shal Marshall & Screws, Berbice, Super Jigga TC aka JaigaTC, Michelle Xavier, Nadia Batson & Patrice Roberts, Ravi B, Erphaan Alves, Fireman, Mikey, Prophet Benjamin, Ann-G, Fya Empress, Lil Bits, KI, Squeeze Head and Shal Marshall, Kernal Roberts, KMC and Ronnie Mc Intosh, 5 Star Akil, Cloud 5, M1 aka Menace, Peter Ram, Hypasounds, Sekon Sta, Preedy, Pternsky, Teddyson John, Ricardo Drue, Voice.

Appendix C (ii)

A Score Sheet of Appearances in the National Calypso King/Monarch Finals (Coverage: 1939, and 1953 - 2016)

Appearances	Artiste
Thirty-Nine Appearances	Chalkdust
Thirty-Eight Appearances	
Thirty-Seven Appearances	
Thirty-Six Appearances	
Thirty-Five Appearances	
Thirty-Four Appearances	
Thirty-Three Appearances	
Thirty-Two Appearances	
Thirty-One Appearances	
Thirty Appearances	
Twenty-Nine Appearances	
Twenty-Eight Appearances	
Twenty-Seven Appearances	
Twenty-Six Appearances	
Twenty-Five Appearances	
Twenty-Four Appearances	
Twenty-Three Appearances	
Twenty-Two Appearances	
Twenty-One Appearances	Sugar Aloes
Twenty Appearances	Cro Cro
Nineteen Appearances	
Eighteen Appearances	Black Stalin
Seventeen Appearances	
Sixteen Appearances	
Fifteen Appearances	
Fourteen Appearances	Duke, Singing Sandra
Thirteen Appearances	Gypsy

A Score Sheet of Appearances in the National Calypso King/Monarch Finals (Coverage: 1939, and 1953 - 2016)

Appearances	Artiste
Twelve Appearances	Sparrow, De Fosto, Skatie
Eleven Appearances	
Ten Appearances	Blakie, Crazy, Brian London
Nine Appearances	Pretender, Bomber, Explainer, Luta, Shadow, Kurt Allen, Devon Seale, Heather Mac Intosh
Eight Appearances	Blueboy aka Superblue, Singing Francine, Karene Asche
Seven Appearances	Melody, Composer, Denyse Plummer, Stinger,
Six Appearances	Spoiler, Young Killer, Kitchener, Tobago Crusoe aka Crusoe Kid, Scrunter, Delamo, Tigress, Roderick Gordon aka Mr. Chucky aka Chuck Gordon
Five Appearances	Christo/Cristo, Striker, Superior, Baron, Watchman, Brother Mudada, Protector, Kizzie Ruiz, Pink Panther,
Four Appearances	Small Island Pride, Calypso Rose, Power, Tambu, Kenny J, Relator, Nap Hepburn, Terror, Bally, All Rounder, Duane O'Connor, Mistah Shak, Queen Victoria
Three Appearances	The Growling Tiger, Cypher, Panther, The Mystic Prowler, Hollis Wright, Johnny King, Maestro, Dougla, King Austin, Penguin, Designer, Valentino, Leslie Ann Ellis,
Two Appearances	Skipper, Spitfire, Yul Brynner/Bryner, Young Creole aka King Creole, Baker, Shorty, Short Pants, Merchant, Machel Montano, David Rudder, M'ba, Kerwin Du Bois, Ella Andall, Sniper, Singing Dianne, Ras Kommanda, Sean Daniel, Twiggy, Alana Sinnette-Khan, Bodyguard, The Incredible Myron B.
One Appearance	Ziegfeld, Atilla The Hun, Eisenhower, Ras Kassa, Caressa, Sir Galba, Dictator, Trini, Syncopator, King Fighter, Tiny Terror, Wrangler, Lion, Caruso, Rikki Jai, Commander, Brother Marvin, Sheldon Reid, Wayne Rodriguez, GB, Roger George, Singing Sonia, Abbi Blackman, Ronnie McIntosh, Eastlyn Orr, Princess Natasha, Buzzing Bee, Conqueror, Crepesole, Funny, Leveller, Poser, Sad Sack, Psycho, Black Sage, Jervae Caesar, Taylor, Maria Bhola, Sekon Alves, Versatile, Contender, Nicole Greaves, Tameka Darius, Benjai, Eunice Peters, Marvelous Marva, Bunny B, Lady Adanna, Helon Francis

Appendix C (iii)

A Score Sheet of Appearances in the Groovy Soca Monarch Finals (Coverage: 2005 - 2015)

Appearances	Artiste
Six Appearances	Shurwayne Winchester, Patrice Roberts, Chucky/Mr. Chucky/ Chuck Gordon
Five Appearances	Destra, Nadia Batson, Benjai
Four Appearances	Biggie Irie, Kerwin Du Bois, Farmer Nappy, Blaxx
Three Appearances	Machel Montano, Denise Belfon, Erphaan Alves
Two Appearances	Blackie, Fay Ann Lyons-Alvarez, Michelle Sylvester, Lil' Bitts, Nnika, Zoelah, Kees, Ravi B, Cassi, Skinny Fabulous
One Appearance	Ainsley King, All Rounder, Blazer Dan aka Blazer, Crazy, Fireball, H20 Flo, Hunter, Jahmoun, Jamsie P, Surge, Johnny King, Keishea Stewart, Kerwin Du Bois & Shal Marshall, Mr. Dale, Megan Walrond, KMC, Metro, Mini Priest, Drupatee, Kerwin Du Bois & Farmer Nappy, Nesta Boxhill aka Sekon Sta, OG, Patch & Mastermind, Yankee Boy and Patch, Peter C. Lewis, Ras Star, Rikki Jai, Skhi, Sean Caruth, TC, Tizzy, Terry Seales, Tony Prescott, Umi Marcano, Tizzy & Richard Trumpet, Zan, Iwer, Zan and Patrice Roberts, Shal Marshall, Super Jigga TC aka Jaiga TC, Tallpree, Mr. Famous, Olatunji, Ricardo Drue, Leadpipe & Saddis, Fadda Fox, Chow Chow, 5 Star Akil, Lyrikal

Appendix D (i)

A Profile of the National/International Power Soca Monarch Winners (Coverage: 1993 – 2016)

Artiste	Number of Wins	Frequency
Super Blue	7	1993, 1994, 1996, 1997 [Tied with Ronnie McIntosh], 1998, 2000, 2013 [Tied With Machel Montano]
Machel Montano	5	2011, 2012, 2013 [Tied with Super Blue], 2014, 2015
Bunji Garlin	4	2002 [Tied with Iwer George], 2004, 2005, 2008
Iwer George	3	2002 [Tied with Bunji Garlin], 2003, 2007
Ronnie McIntosh	2	1995, 1997 [Tied with Super Blue]
Kurt Allen	1	1999
Shadow	1	2001
Shurwayne Winchester	1	2006
Fay Ann Lyons-Alvarez	1	2009
JW & Blaze	1	2010
Voice	1	2016

Super Blue, Kurt Allen and Voice each scored maiden victories, claiming their first soca monarch title on their first trip to the finals. Super Blue (Blueboy) was the inaugural soca monarch. Kurt Allen's win was his only Soca Monarch final; he did not defend his title. In 2010 he won the National Calypso Monarch Competition.

Looking at the Groovy Soca category (2005 to 2015) on its own, there are seven maiden winners: Michelle Sylvester (2005), Shurwayne Winchester (2006), Biggie Irie (2007), Fay Ann Lyons-Alvarez (2009), Kees (2011). Machel (2012) and Olatunji (2015).

To date Voice is the youngest Soca Monarch in the history of the competition; he was 23 years old when he won in 2016. Bunji Garlin was 24 when he won in 2002. Shadow was eight months short of his 60th birthday when he claimed victory in 2001. He is easily the oldest to have ever won the Soca Monarch crown.

Appendix D (ii)

A Profile of the National Calypso King/Monarch Winners (Coverage: 1939, and 1953 – 2016)

Artiste	Number of Wins	Frequency
Mighty Sparrow	8	1956, 1960, 1962, 1963, 1972, 1973, 1974, 1992
Mighty Chalkdust	8	1976, 1977, 1981, 1989, 1993, 2004, 2005, 2009
Growling Tiger	1	1939
Black Stalin	5	1979, 1985, 1987, 1991, 1995
Duke	4	1968, 1969, 1970, 1971
Cro Cro	4	1988, 1990, 1996, 2007
Mighty Spoiler	2	1953, 1955
Striker	2	1958, 1959
Luta	2	1994 [Tied with Delamo], 2006
Singing Sandra	2	1999, 2003
Lord Melody	1	1954
Mighty Terror	1	1966
Sugar Aloes	2	2002, 2008
Lord Pretender	1	1957
Dougla	1	1961
Mighty Bomber	1	1964
Sniper	1	1965
Mighty Cypher	1	1967

A Profile of the National Calypso King/Monarch Winners
(Coverage: 1939, and 1953 – 2016)

Artiste	Number of Wins	Frequency
Lord Kitchener	1	1975
Calypso Rose	1	1978
Lord Relator	1	1980
Scrunter	1	1982
Tobago Crusoe	1	1983
Penguin	1	1984
David Rudder	1	1986
Delamo	1	1994 [Tied with Luta]
Gypsy	1	1997
Mystic Prowler	1	1998
Shadow	1	2000
Denyse Plummer	1	2001
Kurt Allen	1	2010
Karene Asche	1	2011
Duane O'Connor	1	2012
Pink Panther	1	2013
Roderick Gordon/Mr Chucky/ Chuck Gordon	2	2014, 2015
Devon Seale	1	2016

In the history of the competition there have been eight golden winners, each having won on their first trip to the finals: Tiger (1939), Spoiler (1953), Sparrow (1956), Dougla (1961), Sniper (1965), Duke (1968), David Rudder (1986), and The Mystic Prowler (1998).

Appendix D (iii)

A Profile of the Groovy Soca Monarch Winners (Coverage: 2005 – 2015)

Artiste	Number of Wins	Frequency
Shurwayne Winchester	3	2006, 2008, 2010
Machel Montano	2	2012, 2013
Michelle Sylvester	1	2005
Biggie Irie	1	2007
Fay Ann Lyons-Alvarez	1	2009
Kees	1	2011
Kerwin Du Bois	1	2014
Olatunji	1	2015

Kerwin Du Bois was victorious on his fourth attempt at the title. The other winners are all "golden monarchs", having being victorious on their first trip to the finals.

Bibliography

Joseph, Terry. "Calypso Monarch Semis Dubbed 'Calypso Fiasco'."
Express 20 Feb. 2006: Page. Print.

Mondezie, Michael. "Achong Song 'Brings the House Down': Maria Bhola is Calypso Queen."
Express 31 Jan. 2007: 7. Print.

"'Fiery' Sparks Soca Monarch Heat."
Newsday 24 Jan. 2008: A18. Print.

Balgobin, Denise. "Cro Cro To Judges: Do What Is Right."
Newsday 3 Feb. 2008: A7. Print.

Balroop, Peter. "Soca Guys Making All The Money."
Sunday Guardian 10 Feb. 2008: News 11. Print.

Bowman, Wayne. "Chalkie Considers Hanging Up Guns."
Express 24 Feb. 2009: 3. Print.

Bagoo, Andre. "TUCO No Calypso Ties."
Newsday 26 Feb. 2009: A3. Print.

http://www.trinidadexpress.com/index.pl/ article_archive?id =137406717
Express 11th November 2007.

Nicholas, Stephon, and Leiselle Maraj. "After Blowing Away Groovy, Power Soca Field: Montano Eyes Historic Hat-Trick."
Newsday 19 Feb. 2012: A 3. Print.

Choy, Darcel. "3-Title Machel: 'I Never Gave Up'."
Newsday 23 Feb. 2012: A 15. Print.

Felmine, Kevon. "London, Aloes, Cro Cro, Make Monarch Final."
Trinidad Guardian 13 Feb. 2012: A5. Print.

Bowman, Wayne. "'Groovy' Giants Do Battle: JW And Blaze Draw Position #1."
Express 14 Feb. 2012: 20. Print.

Maraj, Leiselle and Darcel Choy. "Munroe Wants $6.4M For Soca Monarch Competition."
Newsday 26 Jan. 2012: A13. Print.

Bruzual, Alexander. "More $$ Or No Show."
Newsday 18 Feb. 2012: A8. Print.

Bibliography

Bowman, Wayne. "'No Money, No Show': Calypsonians Demand $1M Prize For Dimanche Gras."
Express. 18 Feb. 2012: 5. Print.

Castillo, Kimberly. "'More Than $1M Next Year': TUCO Bidding For Increased Calypso Prize Money."
Express 20 Feb. 2012: 4. Print.

Newsday Staff. "Sugar Aloes Serenades Kamla."
Newsday 25 May 2012: A5. Print.

Webb, Yvonne. "Borough Day 2013 All About SuperBlue."
Trinidad Guardian 28 Feb. 2013: A11. Print.

Ramdass, Rickie, "Machel Spared Jail."
Express 26 Feb. 2013: 5. Print.

"Anger Over Toilet Paper, Roti Throwing: Not So Sando."
Newsday 5 Feb. 2013: A17. Print.

Bethel, Camille. "Demas: No Excuses Come 2014:
NCC Chairman To Continue With New Dimanche Gras Despite 'Failed' Idea."
Sunday Express 17 Feb. 2013: 5. Print.

De Souza, Janelle. "'False Papers' Makes The Grade: Bodyguard In Kaiso Semis."
Newsday 18 Feb. 2014: A3. Print.

Cuffy, David. "Chucky Dethrones Panther."
Trinidad Guardian 4 Mar. 2014: A5. Print.

Cardinez, Gary. "Back To The Barrack Yard."
Sunday Express 23 Nov. 2014: 11. Print.

Williams, Shirvan. "Montano Promises The Best Of Monk On Machel Monday."
Trinidad Guardian 6 Feb. 2015: A37. Print.

Mondezie, Michael. "Machel Passes Soca Baton: Sets Sights On Grammy Success."
Sunday Express 15 Feb. 2015: News 3. Print.

Burnett, Verne. "No More Power, Groovy Soca Monarch."
Newsday 5 Nov. 2015: A11. Print.

Campbell, Nigel. "No Live TV for Soca Monarch Next Year."
Trinidad Guardian 5 Nov. 2015: A9. Print.

Bibliography

"Breaking News – Machel Montano Guilty on Five Criminal Charges ... To Be Sentenced January 17, 2013." Express 10 Dec. 2012: Web. 25 Jul. 2015.

Doughty, Melissa. "Banned From Calypso Fiesta, 'Skatie' Wins in Court. Judge: TUCO Out of Place." Newsday 31 Jan. 2016: A3. Print.

Mondezie, Michael. "Confusion Over New-Format Show; Police And Security Clash Backstage ... Chaos Reigns At Soca Monarch." Sunday Express 7 Feb. 2016: News 3. Print.

www.ingramcontent.com/pod-product-compliance
Lightning Source LLC
Chambersburg PA
CBHW041432010526
44118CB00002B/51